Par Albert BERNARD
Instituteur
Officier de l'Instruction Publique

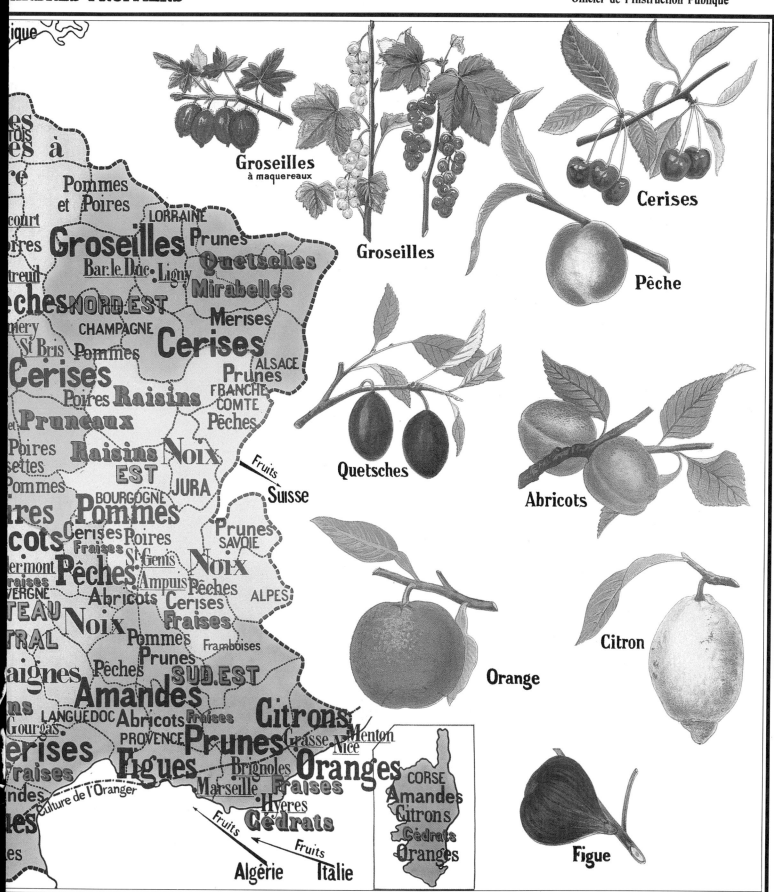

Groseilles
à maquereaux

Groseilles

Cerises

Pêche

Quetsches

Abricots

Orange

Citron

Figue

Pommes
et Poires

LORRAINE

Groseilles

Prunes

Bar.le.Duc .Ligny

Quetsches

Mirabelles

NORD.EST

Merises

CHAMPAGNE

Cerises

St Bris

Pommes

ALSACE

Cerises

Prunes

FRANCHE.
COMTE

Poires

Raisins

Pêches

Pruneaux

Poires

Raisins

Noix

EST

JURA

Pommes

Fruits

Suisse

BOURGOGNE

Pommes

Cerises

Poires

Prunes

Fraises

SAVOIE

St.Genis

Pêches

Noix

Ampuis

Pêches

ALPES

Abricots

Cerises

Noix

Fraises

Pommes

Framboises

Pêches

Prunes

SUD.EST

Amandes

Fraises

LANGUEDOC

Abricots

Fraises

Citrons

PROVENCE

Prunes

Grasse

Menton
Nice

Gourgas.

Figues

Brignoles

Oranges

CORSE

Marseille

Fraises

Amandes

Culture de l'Oranger

Hyères

Citrons

Cédrats

Cédrats

Fruits

Oranges

Fruits

Algérie

Italie

...diteurs, 46, Rue du Bac, Paris

TERENCE CONRAN'S
FRANCE

TERENCE CONRAN'S
FRANCE

WITH PIERRETTE POMPON BAILHACHE
AND MAURICE CROIZARD

DESIGNED BY STAFFORD CLIFF

CONRAN OCTOPUS

I would like to dedicate this book to Michael Wickham and his then wife, Cynthia, who first opened my eyes to the wonders of France on a marvellous holiday in the early 1950s. Since then I've been back often with Caroline and our children for happy holidays in our house in the Dordogne, and recently in Provence – the more we go the more we discover and the more wonderful it seems.

I've also been lucky enough to make frequent visits to Paris to meet with my French colleagues in Habitat and FNAC. They have contributed to the *entente cordiale* and helped me to understand and appreciate *la différence*.

Making this book has been one of the most enjoyable things I have done in my life, and this is partially due to the subject and partially because Hilary Arnold, my editor, has been constantly encouraging. Pompon Bailhache has noted down my long monologues, prodding my memory and filling the many gaps in my knowledge with charm, intelligence, style and patience.

Because Stafford Cliff, my art director, and I have enjoyed the same visual pleasures for many many years, he shared my frustration in having to reject so many beautiful images of France because our book was already full to bursting. But that is symbolic of France.

Terence Conran.

Half title: Pavement café in Lyons.
Frontispiece: Citroën DS at Château de Chambord, Loire.
Title page: A track in Gers, Midi-Pyrénées.
This page: Classic enamelled storage jars.

First published in 1987 by
Conran Octopus Limited
37 Shelton Street
London WC2H 9HN

ISBN 1 85029 050 4

Typeset by Tradespools Limited
Printed and bound in Spain by Cayfosa Barcelona.

CONTENTS

FIRST IMPRESSIONS

France has been a great inspiration to me, both in my design work and in the evolution of the Habitat shops. France seems to exemplify a certain approach to life – it has qualities that would make the world a better place, if they were properly understood and adapted to suit the cultures of other countries. In Britain we have certainly altered the way we live over the last three decades and this has happened because France, and much of Europe, has become a closer neighbour, and an increasingly popular destination for holidays. We eat out far more, drink wine and mineral water with food, invest in well-cut clothes and stock our kitchens with French cooking equipment and food. For centuries French style was élitist, mannered, pretentious – it was designed to set the wealthy apart from the rest. But now we have absorbed that other side of France – the ability to make the mundane and the commonplace a real pleasure.

I arrived in France in 1952 when I went abroad for the very first time. The impact of that journey has never left me. I travelled in an old open Lagonda owned by a friend of mine, Michael Wickham – photographer, furniture maker, artist and bon viveur – accompanied by his wife, Cynthia, and my friend, Patricia Lyttleton. Michael was a marvellous guide, with his inquisitive, discerning eye. That holiday gave me a basis for my own approach to design, and later to retailing. It was an education far more important than the years I spent at art school.

When you visit a foreign country, away from the pressures of everyday life, you look at your surroundings in a freer, more relaxed way, absorbing details and appreciating the broader span. In 1952, the impact was all the greater because I came from England at a time when it was experiencing the extreme austerity of post-war gloom. Everything seemed grey, lifeless and mean. France was dramatically different – abundant, sensual, colourful. Although, at the time, France too was enduring a serious economic recession, to my eyes it seemed like heaven on earth.

We drove through Brittany and then spent a lot of time in the Dordogne, staying in the Limousin region at Donzenac where the whole town seemed to be made of slate. Later we stayed with Nancy Cunard in Lamothe Fénelon. In the eyes of a young Englishman who had hardly ever had a sip of wine, she seemed to drink it constantly – the cheapest of rough red which stained her teeth deep purple. She said, 'Darlings, I can't drink anything refined any longer. It tastes disgusting to me. I only really like this.'

I was very young, inexperienced and impressionable, but all the better for it because I wallowed exuberantly in the simplest things. I was too poor and ignorant to rush around, guidebook in hand, and respond to the overblown elegance of historic châteaux or to search out three-star restaurants. That came later! Then I was delighted with a steak pommes frites and a bottle of local wine in a roadside routier. Nothing will ever taste as good again. I took in the excitement, colour and graphic abundance of the street markets, the beauty of shabby exterior decay on rural buildings, the light and texture of the countryside, and the fresh, functional design of everything from advertising typography to enamelled coffee pots. I returned many times to refresh my appetite for France and things French.

When we opened the first Habitat store in 1964, I was, to some extent, selling my enjoyment of France to the British, importing the things I loved. My experienced retail team wanted to arrange one cast-iron pan, perhaps, with one white cup, on a carefully draped, chequered table-cloth, and keep the stock hidden away. I wanted everything out in the shop, stacked to the ceiling. It was unheard of, revolutionary. No, it was how the French had always done it in country hardware shops, allowing well-designed objects to speak for themselves by presenting them en masse – there to be touched, examined and taken home.

This book is not trying to be a comprehensive encyclopaedia, but a visual appreciation, as diverse as the country itself and as biased and selective as a personal view has to be. Here is a slice of France, the things which I most admire and enjoy. I hope you will find that it reflects the essence of France and will give you some of the same pleasure that France has given me.

My lasting memory of that first trip to France in 1952, is of sensuality. Today, one would have to step off an aeroplane on the other side of the world to experience such an impact on the senses. There was a strangely exotic smell which hit me as soon as I set foot on the quay at Calais, later identified as a mixture of strong tobacco, expensive scent and fresh garlic. Another immediate ımpression was of the elegance of the women, whether young and beautiful in high *chic*, or elderly and widowed in black.

The landscape and the architecture did not take my breath away immediately. What did was the abundance and beauty of ordinary things. Vegetables and fruit were piled into huge mounds, creating a spectacle of colour and texture which focused the eye long before one's mouth began watering at the delicious fresh produce. Flowers – great bunches of one type – were plunged into buckets, not arranged in stilted sprays. What appeared to be French abandon in allowing goods to spill over to the pavement was the most generous thing I had seen.

The cheapest café had a simple sophistication, with white porcelain, metal coffee pots, starched linen, tiled floors, marble-topped tables, and classic café chairs. A dish of *bouillabaisse* looked and tasted magnificent, a plate of steak and chips was a revelation to the palate, and a plain croissant with a bowl of milky coffee gave real purpose to the new day. A carafe of wine arrived with any meal and was included in the low price.

Food markets impressed me most. Even today, shopping at a country market is a great pleasure. They prove that the oldest, simplest form of retailing is by far the most attractive and enjoyable. You are part of a social event, made the more exciting for the opportunity to wander around, browse, smell and inspect the goods at will, and go away with baskets full of the finest food you can buy anywhere, knowing it has come directly from local farms.

9

Consider the variety of ancestral blood which has created the various faces of France. When the Romans invaded what is now France in the first century BC, they came across only Gauls and Basques. Their ancestors remain, but over the next 500 years they were joined by traders from Greece and Phoenicia, domineering Germanic tribesmen (including the Franks from whom the country took its name), Norsemen looking for farmland, and ancient Britons fleeing the Vikings who had settled in *Grande Bretagne*. Those who today live in the areas bounded by other countries naturally have the blood and characteristics of these neighbouring nations, but the French Catalonians, the people of Alsace and Lorraine, those of Italian descent near Nice and the Flemish speakers of the north, as well as the passionately independent Bretons and Basques, would ardently defend their claim to be first and foremost French. Today, cosmopolitan France includes large numbers of settlers from abroad, most of them Europeans, especially Portuguese and Italians, as well as people from former colonies in Africa, North Africa and south-east Asia.

If, therefore, anyone should attempt to describe or define the typical French face they could do little more than allude to one type, from one district, in one region. Generalizations may apply to dress and mannerisms, but rarely to facial features. France is a nation of contrasts, contradictions and extraordinary juxtaposition, and this is what is reflected in the faces of its people. In some, one sees the proud sophistication of the most stylish nation on earth, in others, the gentle rural simplicity of a peasant culture.

Here are some fleeting glimpses of France – the type of images that flash in front of your eyes, then leave a print on your memory. They each express something typical and essentially French.

You would probably pass by this Left Bank restaurant (*top left*) vaguely aware that, like a thousand other traditional restaurants in France, it is utterly pleasant to look at. What is so pleasing is the superb quality and colour of the exterior paintwork – the best anywhere in the world. You then catch sight of crisp white linen and pure white porcelain – and you know that if you were to eat there the food would almost certainly be good. Fine wine would be served in a classic carafe, the salad in a solid glass bowl and the charcuterie on a plain white oval porcelain dish. This understated style only enhances, never detracts from, the food. As much of one's enjoyment comes from the elegant simplicity of the surroundings and objects as from the food itself. One very good reason why, no matter how good the cuisine, French food never seems the same outside France.

A French wedding (*centre left*) sums up a very different quality of French life: the love of pomp and ceremony and public display of familial solidarity, seen here as a father proudly leads his daughter to church at the front of a procession of guests.

Serious cyclists – racers after the ultimate goal of physical endurance, fitness and strength – speed across a country stretch of the Canal du Midi (*below left*). While we English tend to amble around on upright bicycles to do the shopping or gently tour some flat terrain, the French cyclist is quite another creature, fiercely determined and competitive, whether his opponent is a steep mountain road or his fellow racer. In his stylish, skin-tight garb, taking no refreshment other than the occasional mouthful of water, he is as much a part of rural France as the Charolais cattle.

A glimpse of two animated women calling to the street (*top right*) may be as commonplace in Amsterdam or the back streets of Berlin, but the French prostitute has a serious reputation to defend as the best in the world. We foreigners have a romantic obsession for the exquisite quality of French food and wine, its pastoral beauty and architectural grandeur, yet the blatant sexuality encountered on the streets and in the nightclubs of Paris is equally highly regarded, though it is anything but romantic. It is the earthy explicitness and glamorous indulgence that we enjoy. The French reputation for taking sex to the height of an art is a very old one, reaching a peak of notoriety in the 1890s, when France exhibited an attitude of sexual liberation in stark contrast to the hypocritical public prudery of Victorian England. Somehow it has endured the global relaxation of attitudes in the twentieth century, and the French have maintained their reputation for superiority in sex.

There is another quintessential French quality in their attitude to children, which encompasses everything from a reputation for excellence in academic education to a sophistication in child-rearing. No family dinner or celebration is complete without the youngest members who are never considered *de trop* on such occasions. The visitor is also impressed by the stylish chic of children's clothes and accessories – even the school briefcase looks suave and fashionable (*centre right*) carried like a knapsack.

The old *vespasienne* or street urinal (*below right*) is fast disappearing, to be replaced by the ubiquitous, concrete and plastic public convenience. It was the public indiscretion of these handsome contraptions that appealed, making the prudish visitor blush. There is only one left in Paris – outside a prison where it was thought inadvisable to place an enclosed, lockable box!

13

The physical beauty of France is a tribute to sensitive human interaction with nature. The centre of Paris was built from natural materials – honey-coloured stone and blue-grey slate – designed to work in harmony, and has been strictly protected from the ravages of industry and high-rise alike. Its roofscape (*top*) seems more like that of a provincial Renaissance town than a major capital city.

Picardy's flat landscape (*above*) is given an even texture and an en-hancing detail by the farmers. The strong winds which howl across the plain are broken by a line of trees and the soil bears the signs of centuries of intense cultivation.

Roads lined with trees (*right*) to protect the traveller from the elements add a subtle human definition to the French countryside. They have a functional simplicity equally well expressed in the graphic lines of the vineyard and the classic Citroën Dyane car.

The cemeteries of any country are a fascination – historically, socially, and simply for their quiet beauty. In France you can discover intricate, delicate wreaths of glass beads threaded on wire; ancient Celtic crosses reminiscent of Scotland or Wales; carefully maintained grave-yards on the perimeter of every country village, and in Paris the most impressive cemeteries.

Père Lachaise was created in Paris by Napoleon who expanded an old Jewish cemetery. Amongst its imposing tombs the last insurgents of the Paris Commune took a final and bloody stand in May 1871, and were buried under the wall against which they were shot. It remains a place of political pilgrimage, as well as for its litany of famous names including Colette, Balzac, Piaf, Hugo, Bizet, Corot, Delacroix, Chopin, Géricault and Jim Morrison.

Right: Traditional glass bead wreaths in the cemetery at Barsac.

Opposite:
Above left: Père Lachaise in Paris.

Above right: Abundant floral tributes in the village cemetery of Tocane St Apre in the Dordogne.

Centre left: Ancient crosses in the cemetery at Arcangues in the Pays Basque.

Centre right: A graveyard for old vespasiennes on the outskirts of Paris.

Below left: A funeral procession through the St Tropez cemetery.

Below right: Oscar Wilde's grave in Père Lachaise.

The bustling street life of metropolitan France.

Opposite: Flame-throwers performing at the Beaubourg, far below the glass-enclosed walkway of Centre Pompidou.

Top left: Musicians entertaining in the arcade of Place des Vosges.

Top right: Fishermen beside the Seine.

Centre left: A game of draughts in the Jardin des Plantes in Paris.

Centre right: Café life on the pavements of Boulevard St Germain.

Below left: Exciting acrobatics at the Beaubourg.

Below right: A Sunday flea market in Marseilles.

Palm trees and café chairs symbolize the good life on the promenade in Cannes.

Friends deep in conversation against a magnificent vista in central Paris – the Jardin des Tuileries, leading the eye down to the obelisk in the centre of Place de la Concorde (originally from Luxor in Egypt) and, beyond that, the end of the Champs Elysées and the Arc de Triomphe.

Eating out on the pavement of Cours Mirabeau in Aix en Provence.

Les Halles as it was before the market was unnecessarily destroyed – a lasting memory of the best of Paris.

THE FACE OF FRANCE

France is a great individual amongst nations. The face she presents to the world is passionate, intellectual, physically beautiful and powerfully influential. The eight countries that abut her borders – Italy, Germany, Luxembourg, Belgium, Spain, Monaco, Andorra and Switzerland – and the four seas which wash her coastline – the Mediterranean, Atlantic Ocean, English Channel and North Sea – are widely divergent and each has its impact. The country they enclose, despite sharp regional differences, is secure in a strong and stable national identity which she has defiantly defended over the years. France is an amazingly divergent collection of regions and people, with dramatic contrasts in landscape and ways of life. The distinction between the town and the country is clearly defined. What unites this diverse country with its boundaries formed by historical developments beyond its own control? More than anything it is an enjoyment of life.

Gertrude Stein noted '. . . when French people are unhappy that is when they are not occupied completely occupied with the business of living which is the normal occupation their enormously occupying occupation and when for one reason or another that is not occupying them they naturally immediately talk about revolution.' And it is this obsession with life that has made France as famous for her cuisine as for her art, as influential in fashion as in politics and as enjoyable a place to visit as it possibly could be. Its pleasures are laid at your feet and you slip into the French way of life with ease.

The French celebrate their cultural élite, but also those who influence life on an everyday scale. Engineers, designers, chefs, journalists are fêted and honoured, as are those who excel as shopkeepers, bakers, builders, artisans, schoolteachers and wine-growers. Many of their national heroes were not born in France – Picasso, Josephine Baker, Cassandre, Jacques Tati are some of this century's – and this receptiveness to outsiders is extraordinary in a nation known for its chauvinism, whose own writers, artists, philosophers and stars of other spheres can equal or surpass the best in the world.

The explanation, I believe, is that France is a nation with a long history of extracting the best from other cultures and giving it universal appeal through adapting and adopting it themselves. Even the Declaration of Human Rights, which the French made in 1789 during the early months of the Revolution, was Anglo-Saxon in origin, but the French made it peculiarly their own. France has also long been a sanctuary for artists and writers, political refugees, oppressed minorities, innovative entertainers and tax exiles – all of whom are absorbed and integrated while still maintaining their cultural identity.

It is her firm roots in a rich historic and cultural heritage, her strong sense of doing things correctly and stylishly, her radical outlook coupled with a deep respect for the past, her energetic pride in all things French, and above all her love of life – these are the elements which give France such a strong national character.

In the huge bay cradled between the coasts of Brittany and Normandy stands a small granite island seventy-eight metres high. Legend has it that in the eighth century the archangel Michael appeared to St Aubert, bishop of Avranches, in a dream and ordered him to build a chapel there. When this later became a Benedictine abbey, another legend tells of a pregnant woman who was caught by the incoming tide on her way to the abbey. Hearing her cry for help, the archangel duly parted the waves to allow her safely across and as a sign of her gratitude the woman named her child, born shortly afterwards, 'Peril'. Thereafter the abbey was known as 'Mount St Michael in Peril from the Sea'.

The sea here is indeed formidable. The spring tides are the strongest in Europe, with breakers said to flow in at the speed of a galloping horse. As well as this, the unwary walker also risks being engulfed in quicksand.

For over a century now Mont St Michel has been linked to the mainland by a causeway, and cars can be parked at the foot of the rock. Approached by a steep road lined with restaurants and souvenir shops, the magnificent abbey buildings span a wide range of religious architectural styles. At the first level are two Carolingian chapels in the Romanesque style; at the summit, a Romanesque abbey church, its spire topped by a figure of St Michael slaying the dragon. The Gothic architecture of the northern façade has deservedly been referred to as 'The Marvel'. It houses the knights' hall, chaplaincy, guests' hall, refectory, store-room, and the cloister with its incomparable purity of line. They were all built in the twenty-five years between 1203 and 1228.

After that the Mount became a military abbey, and throughout the Hundred Years' War (1337–1453) the knight-monks held out against all attacks from the English, who controlled the surrounding mainland. But now it is just one of France's most impressive tourist attractions.

The French landscape is littered with châteaux, palaces, fortresses, country houses and small manors. Over ten thousand of them are officially listed and many others which do not appear in the guidebooks can be discovered by tourists on their meanderings.

They are particularly numerous in Périgord where legend has it that long ago a saint, passing through the region with a sackful of châteaux, slipped while scaling the hills of the Dordogne and his châteaux poured out all over the countryside. The real explanation dates from the twelfth century when the heir to the duchy, Eleanor of Aquitaine, on being rejected by the King of France, instead married the future King of England, Henry II. Aquitaine became an English possession, but its borders were always ill-defined and hotly contested, and this called for solid strongholds on both sides.

The château of Commarque (*right*), now an imposing ruin rising improbably out of a blanket of greenery, was just such a bastion, and played an important part in the Hundred Years' War (1337–1453). Occupied at one stage by the English, it was later recaptured by the Seneschal of Périgord.

Further east, in the Aveyron region, is another fortress, the château of Najac (*above*). It was there, after they had conquered it, that the English signed a treaty of alliance with the Duke of Aragon against the Count of Toulouse in 1185.

Every château has its own tale to tell, be it heroic or romantic. Anet (*above left*), a masterpiece of sixteenth-century Renaissance architecture, was built in Normandy by King Henri II of France for his beautiful mistress, Diane de Poitiers, nineteen years his senior – a very French liaison! Previously she had been one of the favourites of his father, François I, who had already presented her with the château of Chenonceaux, one of the marvels of the Loire.

In 1554 the English ambassador noted of Anet that it was 'full of objects so sumptuous and princely that he had never seen their like'. In those days the carved hounds above the main entrance were mechanically operated and barked every quarter of an hour at the stag, which then kicked its hoof on a bronze plate!

Vaux le Vicomte (*right*), in the Ile de France, was built in the mid-seventeenth century by the fabulously wealthy Nicolas Fouquet, Minister of Finance to the young King Louis XIV. This jewel of classical architecture is set in a park which is itself the finest example of what the masons of the day called 'hydraulic architecture', the aim of which was to achieve a perfect harmony between stone, plants and water.

Unfortunately Vaux did not bring its owner much luck. His mistake was to throw an over-sumptuous party, to which he had the temerity to invite Louis. The King was so inflamed with jealousy at this dazzling display of wealth that he stripped Fouquet of his possessions, had him put on trial, and locked him up in a fortress, where he died in mysterious circumstances. Not surprisingly, it was to Fouquet's architects, masons and gardeners that the King later turned for the creation of his palace at Versailles.

In complete contrast, the fifteenth-century château (*above right*) with its beautiful tiled conical towers which looks down on the Burgundian village of La Rochepot was built by the knight Régnier Pot on the site of a ruined fortress. Destroyed during the Revolution, the château remained a ruin until the beginning of this century, when it was rebuilt by the son of Sadi Carnot, the first President of the Republic, who was assassinated by an anarchist in Lyons in 1894. Beneath its walls lie the slopes of the famous vineyard of the district – the Hautes Côtes de Beaune.

'*Labourage et patûrage sont les deux mamelles de la France...*' (Ploughing and grazing are the two breasts of France...) – so good King Henri IV was told by his minister Sully at the beginning of the seventeenth century. All French schoolchildren know this famous saying, usually recited with a giggle. And over the centuries it has largely held good: even today agriculture accounts for roughly sixty per cent of the land.

Seen from a train, the countryside unfolds with endless fascination. Whatever the season, it appears like a series of geometric drawings created by the little furrowed plots following minute subdivisions of the fertile land. These in turn are underlined and sometimes framed by a network of countless minor roads, many of them, especially in the south, the legacy of the Romans. These abstract patterns denote an abundant cultivation for this countryside is a major producer of cereals, fruit, vegetables, sugar-beet and tobacco, and is of course the home of the vine. Pampered with love throughout the year, in winter its black root-stocks run in neat orderly lines over the earth like a script, bringing a promise of the new growth, the harvest and wine.

Above left: The vineyards of Alsace.

Centre left: A reflective covering protecting lines of growing melons catches the setting sun.

Below left: Winter lavender fields near Mont Ventoux in Provence.

Right: Young vines growing near Ludes in the Champagne region.

Before the introduction of modern building techniques, houses all over the world were made from whatever materials were available locally.

In France the immense variety of the terrain has meant the houses are often totally dissimilar from one village to the next. Sometimes you only have to cross a river or climb a hill to notice changes: you can see how, for example, the soft white stone of the Loire valley, which goes so well with the slate and silver poplars of Anjou, gives way, as the ground rises, to harder darker rock; and how the surrounding woods grow thicker, with chestnut trees appearing, as the grass becomes more lush.

While the pink granite of a Breton cottage harmonizes with the flowering heather in the landscape, its neighbour in Normandy is half-timbered, and the thatch on its roof is cut from a nearby field.

Down in the south in the foothills of the Alps, where villages, houses and châteaux seem to cling to the rocks, you again find building in stone. Here the stone is usually covered in roughcast plaster in natural colours derived from the local soil; this soil also supplies the raw material used to make the curved tiles that cover the roofs.

Whenever this kind of secret relationship exists between a building and its surroundings, whether humble or splendid, there is a natural harmony, and France, in all her diversity, has many such examples to offer us.

Above left: Chapelle d'Eygalières in Provence.

Centre left: A farm near St Léonard de Noblat in Limousin.

Below left: A house near Beynac in the Dordogne.

Right: A schoolhouse near Garentreville in the Ile de France.

Colours vary from place to place, determined by the rock from which the soil is composed. Around the Morvan the lanes are of granite pink, while those of the Auvergne and Brittany are silver-grey, and the footpaths in the Landes glow sandy yellow. They vary too, with the seasons. In the autumn, forgetting about fertilisers, imagine wandering beside a ploughed field whose newly-turned furrows yield glimpses of the most sumptuous ochres and browns. In early summer, contemplate a walk in the blue lavender-strewn hills of the Drôme.

Despite the introduction of modern farming methods, in many regions of France the land is still divided up piecemeal; as a result nature dispenses her touches of colour in small neat shapes and juxtaposes them so cleverly that it is easy to believe that, for example, the brilliant vivid yellow of that field of rape set off by a tree of apple blossom is there simply to delight your eyes.

Left: Provence – late summer vineyards.

Top: Alsace – an apple tree in a rape field.

Above: Provence – an olive tree in a field of lavender.

35

Wild flowers, referred to by the French as literally 'flowers of the fields', are scattered in profusion throughout the French countryside.

Cornflowers (*above left*), redolent of tender innocent romance, reflect the blue in the national flag – the colour also found on the famous Gauloises packet. White, once symbolized by the royal lily, is now thought of more democratically as being represented by the humble marguerite (*centre left*), from which young couples pull off the petals one by one, saying, '*Je t'aime un peu, beaucoup, passionément, à la folie . . . pas du tout*' – a continental variation on the more prosaic English, 'She loves me, she loves me not'. And the red is found in summer poppies (*below left*), dotted all over huge fields of ripe corn, but reminiscent, less happily, of blood spilt on the northern battlefields of the Somme, the Marne and the Meuse.

Flowers that can be a treat to the taste-buds as well as the eyes and nose – orange-blossom, violets, nasturtiums, acacia – add marvellous scent and colour to the scenery. Fields of huge sunflowers (*right*), so dear to Van Gogh, were once used as animal feed, but today are harvested to produce a light cooking oil much favoured by those concerned with their diet.

Flowers are loved all over France; in the villages every house has its hollyhock, and many towns have their names written in flowers for the tourists; a friendly gesture, if not always entirely pleasing to the eye! The lily of the valley has its own festival, celebrated on the first of May, Labour Day, when young people of all ages rise early to gather bunches to sell as button-holes.

But there is nothing to match the flora of the Mediterranean. Even in winter the hills of the south are covered in vivid yellow mimosa, and in summer the fields around the flower capital of Grasse are saturated with colour and scent, from the blooms used to create its world-famous perfumes.

Touraine, the region known as the garden of France, boasts many fine horticultural delights, but surely the most beautiful is the early sixteenth-century garden of the château of Villandry.

Composed of three terraces, at the lowest level is the kitchen garden, containing every conceivable kind of vegetable – except for potatoes, which were not introduced to France until the eighteenth century. In the middle is the ornamental garden, made up of flower-beds designed as symbolic motifs on the theme of love, bordered by clipped hedges of yew and box. At the top level is the water garden, with its huge mirror of water, and adjoining this is an orchard. This superb layout was the work of Italian gardeners brought

back to France by King Charles VIII from his otherwise unsuccessful expedition to assert his rights over the Kingdom of Naples. But it is also very much an expression of the French tradition of gardening.

Over the years the horticultural marvels of Villandry were to suffer major depredations – chiefly in the name of fashion. In the early 1800s, it was ruthlessly dug up and redesigned in the style of a romantic English garden. Fortunately, at the beginning of this century, the new owner of Villandry restored the château, at the same time undertaking the painstaking reconstruction of the garden in its original form, so that today the park at Villandry can be seen in its true Renaissance splendour.

Each year, at the beginning of the summer season which lasts in principle from mid-May to mid-October, thirteen hundred trees are moved in their square white pots from their winter quarters in the magnificent Orangery at Versailles to spend the warmer months in the open air. Their winter residence, built at the end of the seventeenth century by one of the greatest architects of the day, Jules Hardouin-Mansart, is an immense sober classical building with a central gallery extending over 150 metres in length.

This spacious accommodation is presided over by a statue of Louis XIV, whose image is everywhere at Versailles. Here the monarch surveys a rich forest of greenery throughout the colder months; not just orange trees, as you might expect, but palms, pomegranates, eugenias and eucalyptus trees. The most senior inhabitant is an orange tree over three hundred years old, the same age as its home. The oranges it bears are beautiful to look at but, like those of its neighbours, too bitter and stringy to be good to eat.

During the winter the gardeners at the Orangery also play host to visitors from Paris: the orange trees from the gardens of the Elysée Palace. The task of bringing these seasonal guests indoors when the first frosts come and of returning them to the presidential park in the spring is an enormous operation which falls to the army – nice to think they do something really useful for a change!

The Côte d'Azur may not be quite what it was, and some people find the changes rather depressing, but the original appeal is still there. Its special quality lies partly in the pure blue sky, kept clear of clouds by the Mistral, which blows down to the Mediterranean from the north or north-east during cold spells; partly in the exceptional, dazzling light, which suffuses everything, casting a halo round the houses that seem to be carved out of vanilla ice-cream and then painted in primary colours which soon fade in the bright sunlight to blend in with the landscape.

The perfect Mediterranean idyll is a room looking out on to the sea, with whitewashed walls, a terracotta floor, a huge bed with white cotton sheets, and venetian blinds half closed, letting in a few slanting rays of sunlight.

The Provençal coastline begins at the Calanques, whose high cliffs and rocky promontories stretch from Marseilles to Toulon, then continues along the Côte des Maures, with its pointed headlands and beautiful bays, to the natural harbour of Bormes and the bay of St Tropez. Then comes the Côte de l'Esterel, with its purple hills towering over the deep blue Mediterranean. On the way from Cannes to Nice the coastline becomes less wild, until, between Nice and Ventimiglia, at the foot of the chain of the Alps skirted by the magnificent coast road called the Route des Trois Corniches, it opens out into what is truly the French Riviera.

Above left: The cliffs of the Massif de Puget, between Marseilles and Cassis.

Below left: The romance of the Mediterranean.

Right: The view from a temple of tourism – the Carlton at Cannes.

The Côte d'Azur presents a wealth of contrasts, touching the heights of sophistication and the depths of vulgarity, where the chief impressions are of pure blue sky, perpetual sunshine, exquisite villas, gardens bursting with flowers, the odd mountain, the blue, blue sea and mile upon mile of concrete.

One of its jewels is Cannes, where I vividly remember a scene that typified for me the essence of laid-back *chic* and confidence. Sitting at a quayside café, I watched a handsome young man and beautiful young girl emerge from a luxurious yacht at about two in the afternoon, and sit down outside a bistro. They ordered a whole Camembert and a bottle of wine, which they solemnly shared, and then returned to their yacht. It was so simple and *so* stylish.

Cannes was just a small fishing village until, in 1834, it was discovered by Lord Brougham and his London friends. The Croisette and the Carlton were built at the end of the century, and since 1946 the Film Festival has been flooding the town every May with a huge crowd of cinema and showbiz folk, irrepressibly eccentric as ever.

As well as being *the* place to be seen, the Côte d'Azur is also the classic summer destination for holidaymakers from all over France, who come to worship the sun god, cramming themselves into camping sites and besieging beaches, villages and towns. The really affluent arrive by sea in luxurious yachts. The local glitterati in their beautiful properties lock their gates during the peak holiday period and stay by their swimming-pools to avoid the crowds and the appalling traffic which, in towns like St Raphaël, St Tropez and Nice, rivals even the Paris rush-hour.

Opposite:
Left: I know it's impolite to stare, but won't somebody spare me even a glance?

Right: The sea front at Cannes.

This page:
Above: Putting ashore at St Tropez for a quick drink.

Left: The main drag at Cannes. If it wasn't for the traffic, one could really cruise . . .

There are still plenty of people around who were lucky enough to know St Tropez before it was 'discovered', when it was, as Cannes had been, an unspoilt little fishing village. They all have their own personal memories of the place, usually linked to some romantic episode ... the terrace at Sénnéquier, the little restaurants on the quay where you drank *Rosé de Provence* and ate *bouillabaisse*, the beautiful young things who paraded themselves about the place. In the Brigitte Bardot period there were tight-fitting gingham dresses, and the first bikini tops were being discreetly removed on the beaches of Tahiti and Pampelonne, much to the enjoyment of the mosquitoes as well as the male bathers! What everyone remembers are sailing-boats, yachts, warm summer nights, and the first signs of luxury.

In those days the sea and the sun were available there for everyone, because you didn't need all that much money to enjoy this magical village, with its little houses coloured white, ochre and pink, their gardens bordered with hedges of pink laurel, jasmine and honeysuckle; and, high above, the citadel, with its wonderful view over the bay. Today, however, all this seems to serve merely as a backdrop to a contrived theatrical performance. Although the beaches, the *chic* style, the food and wine, the fashion and the sex still remain, there is an artificiality that wasn't present before, when artists like Signac, Matisse and Bonnard, thrilled by the colours, came to paint.

Today St Tropez is a seed-bed of fashion, where designers of *prêt-à-porter* come to seek inspiration and ideas in the quayside cafés; where, on the beaches, the young people stroll shoulder to shoulder, hip to hip, totally nude; where the smell of frying food begins to waft out of tiny little streets at about eight o'clock every evening, and where you sleep to the sound of a thousand discos ... A vital, modern, completely fascinating place, both ghastly and wonderful at the same time.

France is bounded by four different and ever-changing seas, the North Sea, the Channel, the Atlantic and the Mediterranean, providing two thousand miles of infinitely varied coastline. Hence the evocative names which the French have given to various parts of their coast: the Côte d'Opale, with its two headlands, Blanc Nez (*right*) and Gris Nez; the Côte d'Albâtre, with the superb cliffs of Etretat; the Côte de Grâce, ending at the beautiful port of Honfleur; the Côte Fleurie, whose jewels are Trouville (*above centre*) and Deauville; the Côte d'Emeraude, which begins with the ancient privateering city of St Malo, continuing towards Finistère (*above top*); the Côte d'Amour, around La Baule; the Côte de Jade, facing the Ile de Noirmoutiers; the Côte d'Argent (*above*), around Biarritz; and the Côte d'Azur.

As soon as summer comes, the big cities empty and the population of the coastal areas doubles, in some resorts increasing tenfold. Devotees of Le Touquet and Dieppe are not put off by the bracing weather and cold water to be found there, any more than the Normandy drizzle deters those who like the long fine sandy beach stretching past Deauville or Trouville.

Brittany, to the west, is wilder, with little creeks and large beaches separated by cliffs of granite and shale. According to the tourist brochures, the north coast, on the

Top: Boulogne

Above: La Tremblade

Channel, is warmed by the Gulf Stream – but not everyone is convinced, except on sunny days.

On the Atlantic side the weather is warmer: in the Golfe du Morbihan, in the little islands of Noirmoutiers, Ré, Oléron, and in the Bassin d'Arcachon. Further south the sea becomes rough, and all along the Landes it is too dangerous for bathing. Not until you reach the Pays Basque, around Biarritz, does it become tamer again.

Top left: Honfleur

Top right: Ile de Ré

Above: Deauville

Left: Biarritz

Above: Beached trawlers at Loctudy in Brittany.

Right: Oyster farming in the Bassin d'Arcachon in the Gironde.

Opposite: Lamprey pot handmade by this fisherman near Nantes.

There is good fishing off the coast of France, and the occupation has been carried on successfully for centuries. In earlier times the object was merely to feed the inhabitants of the coast, but with new methods of preserving food and improved means of transporting it, coupled with the advent of the trawler, all that has thankfully changed.

France's principal fishing port is Boulogne, followed by Dieppe, Fécamp and Cherbourg in Normandy, St Malo, Roscoff, Douarnenez, Concarneau, Guilvinec and Lorient in Brittany, La Rochelle in the Vendée and St Jean de Luz in the Pays Basque, close to Spain.

The cold waters of the North Sea and the Channel yield herring and mackerel. The Atlantic and the western Channel provide sole, hake, turbot and whiting, but for cod the boats must head for the waters around Norway or Greenland. Sardine, living in warmer water, are fished mainly from the ports of southern Brittany, the Vendée and Aquitaine, while tuna is hunted as far away as Africa.

Last but not least are the *fruits de mer*: shrimps, prawns, *langoustines*, lobsters and crabs, as well as innumerable other species of shellfish. The pot, or basket, used for catching lobster and crab (of which a variation is also used for the eel-like lamprey) looks pleasing enough to us, but for the unfortunate invertebrate it is a one-way street. Predominant among the shellfish is the oyster. These are raised, or farmed, on rocks all along the coastline from Brittany right down to the Pyrenees, and sold to city dwellers from countless stalls.

There is something very French about the sight of a barge drifting slowly along with the current. French films of the pre-war years are full of such images, stemming perhaps from a sense of regret at the way the country's exceptional network of rivers was neglected at the end of the last century in favour of railways and, later, roads.

This river network has, like the road system, its big 'motorways': four great rivers which drain the water of thousands of their tributaries, streams and canals, into four different seas. The Seine, tame and peaceful, is navigable along almost its entire length. The Loire, long and romantic, is the only French river to stretch over a thousand kilometres; when the tide is out huge sandbanks are revealed down its lower reaches. The Garonne can rise and flood quite dramatically; its estuary, the Gironde, makes one think of a great arm reaching inland from the sea. And the powerful Rhône, rising in the heart of the Alps, is France's main producer of energy as it rushes towards the Mediterranean.

Nearly all of France's great cities were built on these rivers or their tributaries: Paris, Rouen and Le Havre on the Seine; Orléans, Tours, Angers and Nantes on the Loire; Toulouse and Bordeaux on the Garonne; and Lyons, Avignon and Marseille on the Rhône. People were working to make them navigable centuries ago, and the first river to be canalized with locks was La Vilaine, in Brittany, between 1539 and 1585. Later the rivers were linked or 'shadowed' by artificial canals, some of which in the course of time actually becoming rivers themselves. With the advent of more modern methods of goods transport, many of the canals were abandoned, but now they are beginning to be restored, thanks to the new interest in ecology and the growing demand for pleasure cruises by boat or barge.

A barge on one of the Loire's canals.

Right: This waterside scene gives a glimpse of a captivating area in Poitou as yet undiscovered by tourists, its meadows lined with poplars, ash and alder. It is the Marais Poitevin, known as 'the green Venice', where yoles, *the small flat-bottomed boats owned by the locals, glide softly over the water. The* marais, *or marsh, has evolved from what was once a huge gulf dotted with islands, that stretched as far as Niort. In time this gradually became silted up, and from the Middle Ages onwards the area was drained and developed by monks from the abbey at Maillezais.*

Opposite:
Above left: A green meadow by the river Saire in Normandy.

Above right: The town of Falloires hugging the shores of Lake Annecy.

Centre left: The river Sioule in the Méandre de Queuille in the Auvergne.

Centre right: The river Lot at Cajarc, a village dear to former President Pompidou.

Below left: The Loire in full flood at Le Thoureil, a charming little town between Saumur and Angers.

Below right: A drowsy afternoon scene by the Rhône.

Above left: There are charming bridges with no history, like the one we see here over the Canal du Midi.

Below left: Others are steeped in history, like the one at Beaugency. Originally Gothic, it provided until modern times the only crossing point on the Loire between Orléans and Blois, and is an important landmark in the story of how Joan of Arc regained the kingdom of France for the Dauphin.

Above right: The fourteenth-century Pont Valentré, which crosses the river Lot at Cahors, is a splendid fortified structure dominated by three towers. It is constructed of Gothic arches, a style brought back to France from the Orient by the crusaders.

Below right: Even more ancient is the Pont du Gard, near Nîmes, city of arenas, and Uzès, a medieval town which prospered greatly during the Renaissance. The building of the Pont du Gard began in the year 18 BC, on the orders of Agrippa, son-in-law of the Emperor Augustus. As well as being a bridge it was also an aqueduct, bringing water from a distant source to Nîmes, a colony which was then in full flower. The bridge is over fifty metres high, and made up of three storeys, the first composed of 6 arches, the second of 11, and the third of 22. This is one of the most beautiful legacies left to ancient Gaul by the Roman legions.

PARIS

My first visit to Paris, when I went with a girlfriend in the mid-1950s, was quite an adventure – very daring. I had no idea what to expect. Luckily I knew a few people in Paris. I had English friends there and thanks to them we found a hotel which was very cheap – full of bed-bugs like all cheap hotels, but wonderful. It was in rue des Beaux Arts, and in those days it was called the Hôtel d'Alsace. Built as a love nest, attributed to the great eighteenth-century architect, Claude Nicolas Ledoux, it was here that Oscar Wilde took refuge in 1900 and here that he died 'beyond his means'. The hotel has since been thoroughly revamped with velvets and brocades and antique furniture, and is called simply 'L'Hôtel'. It is not to my taste, but today you can enjoy a luxurious stay. However, watch out for the bill! In my time there was a little restaurant on the corner, called Les Beaux Arts, I think, where once a week they would offer free Béarnaise sauce with the steak. It was their speciality, and a real treat.

I never stopped walking when I was in Paris. We spent our time just wandering around discovering little streets and squares, anything new. I found everything exciting, as soon as I got away from the imposing avenues that were part of Haussmann's Paris. Designed to be impressive rather than interesting, to me they were just depressing. The Paris I loved was the Left Bank and the Marais. These days all those big green doors are gleaming, but then the paint was peeling and it looked wonderful. There used to be a tax in France on external signs of wealth, which is probably why nothing ever got repainted. This neutrality of colour was one of the things that most appealed to me: the dull grey of the stone and the zinc on roofs. Since Malraux had Paris cleaned up (in the 1960s), you now see the true colour of the stone, a marvellous honey beige.

The Métro is quite remarkable. Much better than our Underground in many ways: cleaner, more efficient, less noisy. But what it no longer has is that distinctive Métro smell that so struck me when I first arrived. Another thing you notice about Paris today is the lighting. There's no other city in the world where the buildings are so well illuminated. Paris by night is superb. With the possible exception of Venice it is the grandest of all cities.

And then there's the Seine. When I first went to Paris, it played a much more important part in the life of the city than it does today. There was a real river culture then. One of the first things that astonished me was the number of fishermen – they were everywhere. And sitting in the middle of the river were the Ile de la Cité and the Ile St Louis – what a discovery! – a real town within a town.

On those early trips to Paris, as an Englishman I sensed a kind of coldness in the people. They made you feel foreign, and that you were only tolerated . . . particularly if you had a bit of money. You could see it in their faces. I am only talking about Paris here – it was quite different in the country.

One of my favourite places then, and still is, the restaurant, La Coupole. I always go there when I am in Paris, especially in summer when they have huge bunches of gladioli all over the place. I also like La Closerie des Lilas, and La Lorraine, in Place des Ternes, which is not particularly fashionable, but very nice to go to when you are on your own.

And what of recent changes in Paris? The dull, flat area beyond the Champs Elysées and the Avenue de la Grande Armée, where La Défense was erected, was as good a place as any for a modern development, but how they allowed the Tour Montparnasse to go up is incomprehensible to me. I miss the superb metallic structures of Les Halles, designed by Baltard, which have been destroyed. As for the Pyramid at the Louvre . . . I am not sure. But there's no point in complaining. Doubtless when the Arc de Triomphe was built many people thought it was a monstrosity; and the idea of building the Eiffel Tower was completely mad, but if it were taken away from Paris now it would be disastrous. You have to be open-minded. I'm all in favour of new, spirited developments, but only if they are treated with sensitivity.

A Pierre Cardin hat, a helicopter,
and Paris . . . ooh-la-la.

In 1989 the international symbol of Paris, the Eiffel Tower, will be one hundred years old. When it was first erected, its designer, Gustave Eiffel, was universally criticised. Three hundred outraged writers and artists of the day, including Maupassant, signed a protest, attacking it, and in 1907 there was even talk of dismantling it. But, gradually, painters like Dufy, Seurat, le Douanier Rousseau and in particular Robert Delaunay, as well as poets like Apollinaire and Cocteau, began to realise that the tower did have its charm.

Made up of 150,000 steel sections, the tower weighs 7,000 tons (actually very little in proportion to its size) and requires fifty-two tons of paint every seven years. Until the construction of the Empire State Building in 1931, it was the tallest building in the world, and today, with the radio and television transmitting equipment it supports, stands 320.75 metres high.

Right: Gustave Eiffel (in the top hat) on the steps of the tower.

Below: The most familiar picture postcard of them all?

Left: 'Champs de Mars, La Tour Rouge', painted by Robert Delaunay in 1911.

The Porte St Denis (*left*), built in the seventeenth century to commemorate Louis XIV's victories in Holland and Germany, originally marked the boundary between Paris proper and the *faubourgs*, or suburbs. In the nineteenth and early twentieth centuries it was a familiar landmark on the Parisians' favourite *promenade*, along the *Grands Boulevards* between Place de la Madeleine and Place de la République. With a height of twenty-four metres it was for many years the tallest arch in Paris, until it was dwarfed by the fifty-metre Arc de Triomphe. Today the Porte St Denis is lost in a sea of traffic, with cars roaring through and round it without so much as a second glance.

The Arc de Triomphe (*right*), at Place Charles de Gaulle (formerly Place de l'Etoile), is second only to the Eiffel Tower as a tourist attraction. At one time there was a plan to build a vast elephant in its place, with ballrooms, cafés and restaurants in its stomach, which might have surpassed even the Eiffel Tower.

The Arc was constructed at Napoleon's command, to be a 'giant altar of the nation', but by the time it was built, thirty years later, the Empire had collapsed and it was Louis-Philippe who finally inaugurated it, in 1836. It is certainly the most solemn of the capital's monuments, rising majestically out of the hub of Haussmann's immense wheel, with its twelve spokes or avenues, one of which is the Champs Elysées. Underneath the great arch are the flame of remembrance and the tomb of the Unknown Soldier. Foreign heads of state visiting Paris come here to pay their respects, and all the big state processions end here. The Arc is the high point of the imposing triumphal route which stretches across Paris in a straight line from Place de la Défense in the west, under the Arc, through Place de la Concorde and Place de la Bastille to Place de la Nation, and on down Cours de Vincennes to the east.

Paris began life as a small island in the middle of a river which had not yet even been christened the Seine. It was the home of the Parisii, a tribe of Celtic fishermen, who lived there in huts until the Gallo-Romans erected their own town on the site, which they called Lutetia Parisiorum. In the fifth century, under Clovis, one of the first kings of France, this island became known as the Ile de la Cité.

Today the Ile de la Cité is still the true heart of Paris, with its cathedral, Notre Dame, towering over the river, the Palais de Justice, the Gothic masterpiece of the Sainte Chapelle, and the Conciergerie, with its pointed towers, where, during the Revolution, the victims of the Terror spent long hours waiting for the tumbrils to take them to the scaffold. It also contains the charming Place Dauphine, opening onto the Pont Neuf, and a beautiful flower market in Place Louis Lépine, which on Sundays becomes a bird market.

Across the Pont St Louis, the little Ile St Louis is a tiny pocket of the seventeenth century surviving intact, or almost, in the midst of the capital's modern bustle. Originally two pieces of land, separated by a channel and known as the Ile aux Vaches (Island of Cows) and the Ile Notre Dame, they were joined together in the seventeenth century to form the Ile St Louis. The area is a rabbit-warren of narrow streets, and along its splendid quaysides are famous old *hôtels*, or mansions, like the Hôtel de Lauzun and the Hôtel Lambert, both built by Le Vau.

Seen from the air, the two islands look like a great ship moored in the middle of the river, secured at the bow by the Pont Neuf in the foreground and at the stern by the Pont Sully. Paris can truly claim to have the most romantic heart of any city in the world.

There are no fewer than thirty-four bridges spanning the Seine, and these are three of the most interesting. The elegant Pont Royal (*above left*) was used by early commuters, members of Louis XIV's household, to cross from the Palais du Louvre to their mansions in the Faubourg St Germain. A little further upstream, still opposite the Louvre, is the nineteenth-century Pont des Arts (*below left*), which was only re-opened to the public in 1986 after several years of restoration work. This is an unusual iron footbridge with a strangely peaceful and poetic atmosphere, and the view from it is magnificent. It faces the dome of the Institut de France, where, every Thursday, the forty venerable '*Immortels*' (as the Academicians are called) tirelessly revise the dictionary of the French language in an attempt to conserve its purity in the face of a continuous invasion of anglicisms!

The Pont Alexandre III (*right*), with its allegorical statues, stone lions and Florentine street-lights, is a masterpiece of turn-of-the-century architecture. It derives its name from the Tsar of All the Russias, who signed a treaty of alliance with France shortly before the bridge's construction. Crossing over it towards the Rive Gauche you come upon, to my mind, the finest classical building in the whole of Paris – the Hôtel des Invalides.

Although the Seine gave birth to Paris and remains its most splendid avenue, its quaysides have been sadly neglected. Of the thirty kilometres of river bank, only about ten are accessible to walkers. A good quarter are sealed off by urban motorways, while warehouses, depots and quarries account for much of the rest. However, there are plans afoot for the old Citroën factory, for the area around the Pont Henri IV, and for the Bercy and Tolbiac districts, where the riverside will eventually be handed back to the Parisians, complete with new gardens and terraces – and maybe some new restaurants as well.

The most famous squares in Paris are the huge crossroads, like Place Charles de Gaulle, from which the great avenues and boulevards branch out like arteries. But no less rewarding are the smaller, secluded squares, often difficult to find but such a delight when discovered. Place des Vosges (*above left*), in the Marais, is a bit of both. It is a monumental square of perfect architectural unity, but can only be reached through tiny back-streets. It looks like a theatre set, consisting of thirty-six houses with identical pink and white façades and grey-blue roofs, built round a large public garden in which the original, but sadly disease-ridden, elms have now been replaced by lime trees. It was France's first real public square, conceived in the early seventeenth century by the town-planner king, Henri IV, and until the Revolution it was known as Place Royale.

Not far away is Place de la Bastille (*centre left*), a truly historic crossroads. A symbol of the hated establishment, the Bastille was an ancient prison until 14 July 1789, when the people of Paris took it by storm and burnt it in the first major act of the Revolution.

Place de la Concorde (*below left*) is not only the greatest square in Paris but one of the most beautiful in the world. With its mansions built by Gabriel, its statues and fountains, its gardens of the Champs Elysées on one side and the Tuileries on the other, and, right in the middle, the obelisk from Luxor, it brings to mind the carriage-and-four period of the Belle Epoque. It is hard to believe that it was here that the guillotine was erected two hundred years ago, hungrily claiming its 1,384 victims.

By contrast, on the other side of the river near St Germain des Prés you will find a tiny, incredibly peaceful square, with paulownias and white-globed street lamps. This is Place de Fürstemberg (*right*), one of the capital's most charming corners, where the artist Eugène Delacroix had his studio.

I love Place de la Madeleine for the huge diversity of little specialist foodshops, bars and restaurants that surround the classic simplicity of the vast Madeleine.

1 Lucas Carton Once one of the greatest restaurants, and the most beautiful, in Paris. It went into a decline, but was resurrected under Alain Senderens.

2 L'Ecluse Chic and expensive wine bar where you can enjoy a glass of Sancerre and nibble at pâtés and salads.

3 Caviar Kaspia Offers a mouth-watering array of international delicacies to sample – the caviar, and their special vodka, comes from Russia; fat, smoked eel from Norway; smoked salmon from Scotland.

4 Creplet Brussol Stocks over two hundred cheeses, including English ones. Monsieur Lefèvre provides a calendar showing when the cheeses are in season.

5 Maison de la Truffe The Mecca for French cuisine's 'black gold' – truffles. Also sells *pâté de foie gras*, conserves, *cèpes* and *girolles*.

6 Hédiard Sells exotic vegetables and other foodstuffs, and has a fine cellar with a wide-ranging selection of *eau de vie*. They specialize in marzipan and crystallized fruit.

7 Thiebaut Has provided everything for the garden – seeds, bulbs, tools and furniture – since 1857.

8 Fauchon This branch is the *pâtisserie-confiserie*. They make their own chocolates as well as stocking the whole range of French sweets and pastries.

9 Fauchon A paradise for the epicure. All kinds of food from all over the world. Wonderful specialist *charcuterie* and a huge cellar.

10 Ferme St Hubert (21 rue Vignon) A high-class dairy, selling exquisite fresh *fromage blanc*.

11 Le Fournil de Pierre (21 rue Vignon) Cakes, puff-pastry apple tarts, and fresh bread sold by the kilo.

12 La Maison du Miel (24 rue Vignon) Every variety of French honey – enjoy tasting before you buy.

13 Tanrade (18 rue Vignon) Sweets, fruit syrups, *marrons glacés*, and especially jam, including one you won't find anywhere else – made from depipped redcurrants!

14 The flower market Every day, except Sunday, you can find huge buckets filled with glorious, freshly-cut flowers for sale in generous bunches.

In Paris, brasseries tend to be run by Alsatians, while café *patrons* are generally Auvergne men, whose ancestors settled in the capital to sell wood and coal and went into refreshments as a sideline, which gradually took over. It was they who started the custom of setting tables outside on the pavement.

Above left: During the Second Empire there was a draper's shop in the famous angle of the Boulevard St Germain, opposite the church, called Les Deux Magots. It was replaced by this café which became one of the capital's great cafés littéraires, along with its neighbour, Le Flore.

Below left: Recently the traditional Parisian café design has been brought up to date by Philippe Starck, with the Café Costes in Les Halles.

Above right: Even the smallest café, like Le Sauvignon, in the publishing district, shows the care which goes into its design, and the beauty and quality of the materials used, from the zinc bar surface to the humblest chair.

Below right: Literature rubs shoulders with politics in the Brasserie Lipp, which is decorated with Belle Epoque ceramics and usually adorned by a bevy of celebrities. The café was founded around 1870 by an Alsatian, Lippmann, who bequeathed it his name and its famous sauerkraut; but it owes its high reputation since 1920 to a man from the Auvergne, Marcellin Cazes. Thus two traditions overlap.

Shopping is one of the most popular Parisian pastimes, as well as a major attraction for visitors.

Opposite:
Above left: The Avenue Montaigne is the Mecca of fashion, and the star of the show is undoubtedly the Dior shop, painted pearly grey.

Above right: The beautiful Guerlain shop in the Champs Elysées had already been a perfumery for over a hundred years when, in 1938, its famous Institut de Beauté was inaugurated with decor by the great artists of the time – Christian Bérard, Jean Michel Franck and Diego Giacometti.

Centre left: Biberon, in spite of its name, which means a baby's bottle, is a long-established stationery shop.

Centre right: Opposite the Pont Neuf is the great department store, La Samaritaine, an immense edifice of metal, glass and tile.

Below left: Dehillerin, an old and famous ironmonger's specializing in traditional kitchen equipment, was an inspiration at the start of the Habitat shops.

Below right: Many small shops have brightly painted metal security screens which produce that familiar clattering sound in the mornings.

This page: Another of the great stores is Galeries Lafayette, whose huge cupola is so typical of the wrought-ironwork of the early twentieth century when it was built. Stores of the future would do well to note the glamour these shops offer their customers.

Every year, twice a year, Paris is invaded by the world's fashion pundits, desperate to see the next season's clothes designs. Excitement sends an electric charge through the crowd, crammed together for the show – sweat and scent, heat and light intermingle. As the pulsating music begins, the flashbulbs explode and the magnificent models prance into view revealing the latest secrets of a great designer.

Inflated egos dominate the scene. Every designer has his coterie of famous followers, and every fashion editor an entourage of assistants. Behind the scenes the craftsmen in the ateliers of the great fashion houses have worked almost without sleep for months, perfecting the clothes. Money lubricates this major French industry – the world's top designers are amongst the most internationally successful business names, their empires based on dressing the small number of extremely wealthy women in the world who can afford excessively expensive *haute couture*. From a core of élitism, the empires branch out into *prêt-à-porter* clothes, perfumes and labelled accessories from scarves to luggage. Pierre Cardin, the richest designer, has his name on 840 licensed spin-offs, including a tin of sardines, and Yves Saint Laurent has a brand of cigarettes among his 211 licences.

Yet the reason behind Paris's domination of world fashion is not the power of money, but the staying power of its designers who have consistently kept France in the forefront of fashion, despite challengers in New York, Milan and London. They may have great designers too, but no other city can compete with the tradition of Paris fashion, its roll-call of great names and, above all, its ability to go on producing simply the best cut, best made, best promoted and best sold clothes on earth.

Emanuel Ungaro's show held at the Grand Hôtel in 1985.

To the north-east of Paris, on the site of the old abattoirs of La Villette, stands an enormous silver sphere, made of 6,433 triangular, stainless steel mirrors. It is La Géode (*left*), symbol and beacon of the new Cité des Sciences et de l'Industrie.

This immense shop window on the future, with its Planetarium, Vidéothèque, Inventorium (for children), and an area called 'Explora', was opened in the spring of 1986 as a sort of permanent exhibition, covering thirty thousand square metres on three floors.

Adrien Fainsilber's architectural masterpiece includes a 370-seat 'multimedia' auditorium, the only one of its kind in France; above it is a screen of perforated aluminium twenty-six metres in diameter which plunges you into picture and sound by means of hyper-sophisticated techniques. The films that are shown – 'Water and Man', 'Chronos' and 'The Dream is Alive' (shot by the space shuttle astronauts in flight) – make you feel you are actually taking part in the adventure. You fly over mountains, plunge into precipices, feel the earth fall away from under your feet, and emerge terrified but elated. Numerous school parties come to La Géode, and of the three-and-a-half-million visitors in its first year about two-thirds were children.

During the 1950s tower blocks began to spring up to the north-west of Paris, just beyond the Pont de Neuilly. 'A mini-Manhattan on the doorstep of Paris' was the builders' dream. This was the France of tomorrow that, thank God, no one yet dared to build within the capital itself, and so La Défense was born.

Here, behind a fifteen-metre high, abstract steel sculpture by Calder, we see the Fiat tower (*right*), which has forty-six floors, twenty-two lifts, and houses 4,500 employees. This is a second-generation tower, fourteen years younger than the Nobel tower which represented the first generation. Today it is the third-generation Elf tower, 180 metres high, that dominates this gigantic complex covering 1,800 acres and the areas of Courbevoie, Puteaux and Nanterre.

The new city's first building was the CNIT (Centre National de l'Industrie et de la Technique), an exhibition hall built in 1958. Although the incredible span of its concrete roof has never yet been surpassed, today it seems dwarfed by these modern giants.

Thanks to the RER, La Défense is less than fifteen minutes from the centre of Paris, and more than 100,000 people now work there. However, despite its painstakingly-designed green areas, commercial centres, restaurants, sports facilities and underground railway network, rather fewer people live there; for while La Défense is already one of the foremost trading centres in Europe, its 'modernist' affectation makes it slightly ridiculous, and it has failed to become a real town.

The Beaubourg (*below left*), more correctly the Centre Pompidou, celebrated its tenth birthday on 2 February 1987. This doesn't prevent some Parisians from still referring disparagingly to it as 'the factory' or 'the refinery'. For them the Beaubourg's huge, bright blue ventilation pipes, its 150,000 tons of steel and 50,000 square metres of concrete, and the square in front of it milling with buskers are an eye-sore and a disgrace to Paris. Many of the objectors, of course, have never set foot inside it – they don't know what they are missing. The figures speak for themselves: 25,000 people visit it every day, making it the most visited cultural centre in Paris, possibly in the whole world.

It has housed several famous exhibitions, notably the Paris-Moscow, Paris-Berlin, and Vienna, but it is also a place people come to for no particular reason – just to be there. It is a museum which doesn't *feel* like a museum, and has breathed new life into the Marais, which had become little more than a museum itself. And from the top, which you reach by a series of escalators sheathed in transparent plexiglass tubes, there is a staggering view of Paris.

Not to be outdone, the venerable Louvre Museum is also being revamped. The basement is being refurbished, escalators are being put in, and the Ministry of Finance banished from the part of the building that is

on the Rue de Rivoli. Naturally, controversy rages here too, its main focus being on the thirty-two metre high transparent pyramid (*above left*) designed by the Chinese architect Iech Ming Pei, which is to be built in the centre of the Cour Napoléon to light the future central hall. The people of Paris have been shown a model of it, but they are not entirely convinced. . . .

The opening of the Musée d'Orsay (*above right*) at the end of 1986 also caused quite a stir. The former station, built around 1900 (and actually rather fine, though for a long time it was considered an awful heap), is now dedicated to the art of 1848–1914. Not everyone agreed with the concept of putting Monet and Detaille side by side, the classic with the avant-garde, but the public has a right to judge for itself what history has already passed judgement on. And there is obviously no reluctance to give it a try, since there is always a huge queue to get in.

There is one museum, at least, that everyone is happy about, or has been since its opening in September 1985. The seventeenth-century Hôtel Salé (*below right*), a former residence of the nobility of the Marais, now houses an important Picasso collection, accepted by the state in lieu of death duties. It is hard to imagine a happier marriage of past and present. Picasso seems quite at home behind his Louis XIV walls.

Although it doesn't often happen, Paris seems made to be seen in the snow. The addition of white lends even more aristocratic beauty to the fine stone façades of the buildings, already very smart thanks to meticulous scraping during their compulsory clean-up during the Malraux era. Suddenly all the soft neutral colours stand out – the ivories, the various shades of grey in zinc and slate, and the deep, sombre green of the huge carriage-gates.

It is in the parks and gardens that the snow really adds an extra dimension. The light changes from a very soft yellow to the palest of blues, and the city's basic colours are revealed. The ponds freeze over, and the countless Parisian sparrows go in search of crumbs; by a miracle of nature their own special metabolism protects them from the cold.

These unfamiliar scenes, and the muffled stillness of the side-streets, are a feast for the senses, and should be savoured while they last. By tomorrow it will all have melted, and the pavements will be covered with slush. Then you will see the valiant street-sweepers, many from North Africa, shivering through yet another European winter....

Saladfes

Hanicot vert fils

Scarole

mange-Tout

RURAL LIFE

RURAL LIFE

If you ask any French city dweller about their roots, even the most sophisticated will almost certainly say that at least one of their grandparents was a peasant. In a generation's time, however, this will no longer be the case. At the turn of this century half of France's population cultivated the land, but today this figure has been reduced to about eight per cent. France is sparsely populated in comparison with all its immediate neighbours and since the Second World War the cities have swelled while the countryside has emptied. Successful economic growth has resulted in a massive increase in urbanization.

The changes in farming methods and distribution have also been radical, with agricultural production climbing continually. The image of France as a nation of small farmers subsidised by the European Economic Community and immune to modern economic pressures is not wholly true. Increasingly, traditional small-holdings are being grouped into large properties, often jointly owned by co-operatives. While in the 1930s a farm of fifteen hectares was regarded as sizeable, today an area of eighty or so hectares is generally considered the minimum from which one person can earn a living. French farmers have to resist the invasion of imported food, often taking direct action by blocking roads with their tractors, sometimes dumping huge mounds of artichokes and tomatoes they have grown but been unable to sell, in an attempt to prevent Italian wine, English lamb or Spanish vegetables reaching the French household and undermining their livelihood.

Despite these developments, for the visitor from abroad rural France has lost little of its appeal. Influenced by a romanticized vision presented in books, films, paintings and magazines, we tend to have an idealised view of French country life, but in fact the reality rarely lets us down. There remain pockets where you can feel you are living in a different age, where the peasant appears to continue cultivating the land exactly as his father before him, and village life goes on as it has for centuries. My house in Provence is surrounded by hay meadows and olive groves looked after by one man. He works seven days a week, beginning at seven in the morning and is frequently still harvesting the hay as darkness falls. Very often he returns at midnight to regulate the flow of the little brooks that irrigate his fields. It is difficult to imagine that a young man, accustomed to a thirty-five hour working week, is going to be eager to take his place in the future.

The French seem to have a deep instinct for cultivation, with small-holdings and tiny vegetable gardens abounding through the country, begging the question, 'Is it really worth growing tomatoes when they can be bought in great abundance at the local market for very little?' The answer is clearly 'yes', maybe as much a result of French frugality as of the sheer enjoyment of growing and eating garden-fresh food.

While the great towns and cities of France were built to impress, the physical beauty of the village is on a smaller, more domestic and welcoming scale, and this carries through to the people who live there. Although the regional variations in village life are enormous, they have in common the fact that the shops, markets, cafés and municipal buildings are social centres where people take time to discuss their village life and ignore the world beyond.

Tradition is the key to our love of rural France. We enjoy nothing more than observing the rituals of the country markets and shops. The nation's outstanding cuisine is based upon the quality of the raw ingredients, the best of which are still grown and manufactured using traditional methods, and sold in small quantities as regional specialities. We take many traditional French country objects into our homes and are influenced by the pace and way of life when we introduce pavement cafés and garden furniture into our lives. Even the denim we wear originated in a southern French town.

Rural France is still as enchanting as the photographs in this book illustrate, which, if anything, understate its beauty and particular ambience, and, sadly, cannot bring you the wonderful smells which pervade any journey through the French countryside.

The popular image of the French peasant, in a black wool beret and heavy-duty blue cotton overalls known as *bleu de travail*, has become a visual cliché of rural life in France. Although you still see *bleu de travail* in many areas of France, they are swiftly being replaced by the ubiquitous denim jean.

Blue jeans became highly fashionable in the United States in the 1960s, when stars like Marilyn Monroe, Marlon Brando and James Dean first wore them on screen, and soon they crossed the Atlantic to achieve the same cult status in Europe. Most people in America are aware that blue jeans were invented there in the mid-nineteenth century by a young man called Levi Strauss, who sold his hard-wearing trousers initially to gold prospectors. What most Americans and others don't realize is that the tough jeans cloth originated in France.

Nîmes, in the South of France, had long been the centre for the weaving of a thick, tough cotton fabric called *serge de Nîmes*. It was usually dyed indigo blue and used for making tarpaulins. After much experimentation, Levi Strauss decided to use it to make his trousers and it soon became known as 'denim'.

The distinctive look of blue jeans — tight-fitting, low-waisted, narrow-legged, with copper rivets and orange stitching — was created at a time when every French peasant was still wearing baggy brown corduroy trousers and *bleu de travail*. It has taken over a century and a half for the cloth from Nîmes to become fashionable at last in its country of origin and, ironically, to begin to replace the traditional uniform of the French countryside.

Above right: A barn in Alsace.

Centre right: Peasants at Salon de Provence, Bouches du Rhône.

Below right: A Pyrenean shepherd.

Left: A cooper at work in the Cognac region, and bleu de travail.

In France every village worthy of the name has a church tower, and more often than not the houses are clustered around it. In front of the church, the market square provides the focal point of the village. Probably shaded by plane trees, limes or chestnuts, it is the setting for the *café de la place*, where in fine weather the villagers sit with their apéritifs.

Until quite recently village life was punctuated by the ringing of church bells, and today, even in parishes that no longer have a curate, the bells still sound the alarm in case of fire or other emergencies. The bell-tower is topped by a weather-vane,

usually in the form of a cockerel, which people still use as an indicator of wind direction and a guide to forecasting the weather.

Naturally not all villages conform to this pattern. In south-western France, for instance, there are villages called *bastides*, fortified by the counts of Toulouse against marauding English soldiers from the adjoining region of Aquitaine, once an English possession.

Top: Roussillon in Provence.

Above: A village in the Tarn valley.

Right: A bastide in Gers.

94

The picturesque village of Riquewihr in Alsace.

La Roque-Gageac, clinging to the side of the gorge along the river Dordogne.

96

Provenchère, a hilltop village in the Haute Saône.

A wintry scene near Bourg St Maurice in Haute Savoie.

Maussane and Paradou are my local villages in France. They merge together along a shady road lined with plane trees and provide the local inhabitants with a cornucopia of shops, services and visual pleasures. The residents are traditionally involved in various agricultural activities such as olive growing, wine making and the cultivation of fruit and vegetables. This is the area for the *primeurs* – the first young vegetables available in early spring. They are usually grown in polythene tunnels shielded from the withering Mistral by row upon row of neat, dense cypress trees. White and mauve asparagus abound at Easter, followed by the first peas and courgettes. Early summer brings vast crops of cherries and, soon after, apricots, and then it's the peach and melon season. With the first really hot sun come the wonderful, juicy tomatoes and garlic – mounds of it, strings of it, mountains of it. Garlic forms the cornerstone of Provençal cooking and is on everyone's breath. By midsummer, aubergines and green and red peppers join the tomatoes, courgettes and garlic and the local olive oil to make the most typical and sustaining of Provençal dishes – *ratatouille*. The local wine is usually *Rosé de Provence* – not a great wine but clean and very refreshing; just the right accompaniment to the climate and the aromatic food.

D 78^c

MAUSSANE
LES ALPILLES

Top: An olive grove backed by the Alpilles.

Above: Visitors are kept well-informed by this street map of Maussane.

The backdrop to this highly productive vegetable garden are the rocky Alpilles hills, carved into strange sculptural shapes by the fierce Mistral. These tiny mountains are covered in the herbs – wild thyme, rosemary, marjoram and fennel – whose flavour seems about four times more intense than usual and scents the air, the food and the flesh of the animals that graze on the slopes.

Huge amphitheatres and forums, and crumbling aqueducts traversing the countryside, bear witness to the Roman occupation of the area. Bullfights, or, rather, non-aggressive teases, are a local summer sport.

The quality of light in the region is remarkable, as both Cézanne and Van Gogh appreciated, and encourages the best from artists and photographers. You can see why I live here despite the tourists, the mosquitoes and the Mistral.

Above: Somehow the signs seem to add charm rather than detract.

Below: White bands on trees aim to keep the night driver on the road, not always with success.

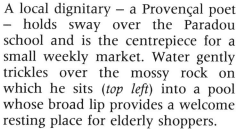

A local dignitary – a Provençal poet – holds sway over the Paradou school and is the centrepiece for a small weekly market. Water gently trickles over the mossy rock on which he sits (*top left*) into a pool whose broad lip provides a welcome resting place for elderly shoppers.

The townhall or *mairie* (*centre left*) is a real 'communal house' for Paradou, displaying announcements of births, marriages and deaths on its rather grand gateposts.

The church of Maussane (*below left*), originally a Romanesque building, holds centre stage for Maussane's weekly market. God and commerce seem in total sympathy here.

Man and Woman's spiritual needs and bodily functions are displayed in a charming and unselfconscious juxtaposition (*right*). The church is quite at home amidst market stalls so it seems equally natural to erect Christ on his cross by the public lavatory.

Though it only numbers about a thousand inhabitants, this small community supports four restaurants, two hotels, two cafés, four bakeries, two butchers and three antique shops, not to mention a hairdresser's, a chemist, a photo shop, a library, a general store, a launderette and two small supermarkets including the 'Casino' (*above right*). The twice-daily purchase of bread is an important factor of village life, and one of the bakeries (*top left*) also does a thriving pâtisserie trade, especially on Sunday mornings. This excellent butcher's shop (*top right*) sells delicious joints of mountain lamb, fed on the abundant herbs of the Alpilles, and plump juicy rabbits – a delicacy of the area – as well as fresh pasta. Huge jars of dried *cèpes* and *morilles* stand on the counter. The video shop (*above left*) keeps the village in touch with modern life with the latest movies.

The olive oil co-operative (*top left*) presses the farmers' olives and sells the greeny-gold oil in vast, rather unromantic five-litre plastic cans. This is quite simply one of the best, and most expensive, olive oils in the world. From one of the local tourist shops, where it appears in pretty litre bottles with dainty labels announcing 'extra-virgin olive oil, first pressing, from Maussane, Provence', it costs even more. Market day is the high point of the week, when the stalls set up in the square around the church (*above right*). A vast range of farm produce is displayed, alongside excellent charcuterie (*above left*) as well as clothing, flowers, antiques, pottery and hardware. God must be happy to see Man rejoicing in his wordly goods. Maussane also boasts one of the prettiest petrol stations in France (*top right*), with a wonderful balcony of pelargoniums and geraniums and a fine old rusted tractor.

Pétanque, or boules, is played on Maussane's gravelly dirt pitch in the market square. The players may then adjourn to their favourite café to quench their thirst, celebrate success or drown their sorrows.

The villages have a plethora of cafés each popular for some indefinable reason with its own loyal clientèle. The Café de la Fontaine faces the main square in Maussane.

While the men play pétanque, some wives congregate in one of the wash-houses. This huge, cool one was built in Napoleon's time, but sadly, since the advent of the washing machine, is no longer the popular meeting place it once was.

The Café du Commerce where many a glass of 'pression' beer is downed after a hard day in the fields.

As the old-fashioned methods of farming gradually die out, it is still possible, in certain parts of France, to see picturesque evidence of archaic habits lingering on – a team of oxen, for example, or a cart-horse slowly working its way across a field. Luckily for France's standing in the European agricultural community, you won't find these relics of the past round every corner!

The average size of a French farm is still only about sixty acres. Half the agricultural land is owned by peasants, and therefore cultivated directly by the land-owner. But nowadays owning the land you cultivate is no longer enough to guarantee you an adequate income. In fact, the farmers of the large concerns around the Paris area, who own only their livestock and machinery, not the land itself, tend to be better off than the owner-occupiers of southern and south-western France.

Some of the poorest agricultural areas in the country are those where farmland is still divided up into small fields, separated by hedges and trees. It used to be quite common for one farmer's plots to be scattered about at random, often far apart. This arrangement, although beneficial to the ecology with its network of hedges, is less good for the farmer, as it wastes space, makes more work and impedes the use of tractors.

The regrouping of lands has greatly altered the look of rural France. Those tiny fields, however, where they still exist, produce vegetables more succulent than you will find anywhere else.

Above right: Making hay the mechanical way in Normandy.

Centre right: The way they do it in the Pyrenean valley of La Barousse.

Below right: Planting cabbages in St Donat sur l'Herbasse, Isère.

Left: Horsepower, old and new, in the Loire valley.

An ancient French gardening manual begins: 'The crops, once seeded and planted, must be successfully brought to fruition by the vigilant offices of the gardener.' That done, once they are harvested some crops still need to be dried. Garlic is left hanging, head down, for several weeks before being plaited by its tail into a neat tress. Another is tobacco, which, as a state monopoly, is strictly controlled and cannot be planted without a licence nor privately sold.

The blue plums of Agen become *pruneaux*, much sought after for their delicate taste, despite their huge stone. They can be stewed, perhaps to nestle in the centre of a crown of *riz à l'impératrice*, a delicious creamy dessert, or made into a stuffing for a Breton *boudin* (black pudding).

Chicory (*endive*) is a winter salad crop which grows in the shade. The French often liken sickly-looking people to this pallid plant. Children who grow tall too quickly, on the other hand, are taunted with looking like an asparagus (*asperge*). As soon as the plant has pushed its pink tip out of the sandy soil in which it thrives, it sends its aristocratic-looking stalk shooting up towards the sky. It is harvested as soon as the first buds appear on the tip. The early crop comes towards the end of March or the beginning of April, with a later one in July and August. The humble leek, meanwhile, is sometimes referred to in France as 'the poor man's asparagus'.

Above left: Packing asparagus.

Below left: Garlic peeling at Tournecoupe in Gers.

Top right: Tobacco leaves hanging up to dry in the Cher.

Centre right: Racks of Agen plums.

Below right: Sorting chicory at Yvelines.

For at least seven centuries Normandy has been producing cider. From its many orchards, which blossom so enchantingly in spring, come both sweet and bitter apples, which are used in varying proportions to make *cidre doux* (sweet cider), *cidre bouché* (fine bottled cider), and even a *cidre mousseux*, which sparkles like vintage champagne.

If cider is distilled it produces an eau-de-vie which is equally famous, if not more so – calvados, popularly referred to in France as *calva*. Heavy eaters have been known to use this to produce *le trou normand*, in other words, to pep up their jaded appetites between courses!

Above: Cider apples stored in a loft.

Left: A traditional cider press.

Opposite above: A Norman cider farm.

Opposite below: A calvados label.

111

All over France you see little kitchen gardens dotted about the place, right up to the outskirts of the big cities. Their eye-catching red tomatoes and borders of vivid green parsley seem to have the primary purpose of exciting the appetite, and the vegetables produced from their flowering rows of beans and peas are unbeatable when served freshly picked at the family table.

All the gardener needs for this pleasant enterprise is a very small plot of land. There are indeed more kitchen gardens than flower gardens in France, though flowers are by no means neglected: they are often so harmoniously interspersed with the vegetables that it is hard to tell the difference between a functional garden and a pleasure garden.

Top: Allotments on the outskirts of Cordes in Tarn.

Above: A kitchen garden in Taninges, Haute Savoie.

112

It is not enough simply to sow the seeds: every garden is different, and needs tending accordingly. Above all, the gardener has to know how to handle the land, to get it into peak condition and keep it that way month after month. He must take into account how much sun the garden gets and which way it faces – sometimes the end result is a charming terrace or espalier. Space must always be found for the herbs which play such a vital part in French cuisine: sage, for enhancing the flavour of game; rosemary, for fish and grilled meat; thyme, for sauces; chives, the perfect accompaniment for soft white cheese; anise, to flavour and help digest fatty dishes; and melissa, or lemon-balm, whose bitter taste goes well with salad.

There is no record of the amount of food produced by France's kitchen gardens, but their surplus is often on offer at country markets. It is not unusual to see as little as three bunches of vegetables for sale on an upturned crate.

Left: Terraced cultivation at Lyas in the Ardèche.

Below: A country market in the Vaurais village of Bessières.

Every farm has its own individual character. Its size and importance should never be gauged by the scale of its living quarters. These may be quite modest, while the granaries and stables are large and full, the land extensive and productive.

The small farmsteads which have been handed down from generation to generation nearly all show traces, behind the corrugated iron and concrete, of the simple, charming rural architecture which, it goes without saying, was based on local materials. In some areas the farms stand out alone and isolated; in others they are grouped together in hamlets. Originally these would have belonged to members of one family who, through the vagaries of inheritance, had no choice but to share the land out among themselves. Sometimes even the living quarters of a farmhouse are divided in two. These hamlets, and sometimes the whole locality, usually bear the name of the original family. They all appear on the Michelin maps, where they read like a litany of rural family names.

No farm, even a large wine-producing concern, is complete without its own chickens, feeding on grain and purging themselves with bitter green grasses. There is nothing to compare with the flavour of a freshly-laid free-range egg, and the plump young chickens are delicious.

Top left: An old farm built of stone and clay.

Centre left: A small farm near Morgat in Brittany.

Below left: A wine-producing farm near Béziers in the Languedoc.

Right: Time stands still in a farm hamlet at Ostabat in the Pyrenees.

Moving livestock about is no joke these days. Even though most farms are connected to their pastures by a network of tracks, sooner or later the farmer has to use the public highway, even if it is a major road. In the areas where livestock abound, the motorist has to be on his guard, and ready to slow down to a halt. Just around the next bend you are liable to come across a flock of nervy sheep – or something heavier.

A by-product of the ecological movement in France is that many young people are putting themselves forward to become shepherds or shepherdesses. To a city dweller this may seem a romantic way to get back to nature, but in the country it is common knowledge that shepherding is particularly arduous work. The shepherd has umpteen problems to contend with, from the cruel viruses that attack the animals to the difficult births that place the lives of ewes and lambs in danger.

Perhaps the root of the attraction is the image, ingrained in the French consciousness, of Queen Marie Antoinette dressing up as a shepherdess in the Petit Trianon. This may help to explain why fewer people apply to tend oxen or geese! Not that geese really need anyone to guard them: they are happy just to follow their leader, who waddles along, cackling away, and good luck to the unsuspecting cyclist or walker he meets on his way. The moment he feels threatened he will stick out his long neck and give a horribly painful bite with his beak to any unwary leg that comes within range.

Left: A shepherd and his flock in the Haute Loire.

Top right: A powerful team on the Cotentin peninsula in Normandy.

Centre right: A gaggle of geese in the Dordogne.

Below right: Short back and sides in the Cévennes.

Above: A Portuguese worker tends hens in the Chartres area.

Right: Milking time in the Auvergne.

Intensive, small-scale farming is fast disappearing in modern France. 'Nowadays you can't make a living with only one or two animals,' ruefully comments an old peasant in a poor region of central France. Yet there are still a few like him, whose principal source of income is the cheese made from the milk of a modest herd of goats or a couple of cows. The *fromages frais* they produce are exquisite cheeses, still sold at village markets resting on a vine or cabbage leaf, alongside other delicious animal products. All are made locally on small holdings by peasants whose methods of work have remained unchanged for centuries, continuing a tradition of fine food unequalled by modern methods of mass production.

Above: Open air and individual attention for a herd of pigs at Allanche, in the Cantal region.

Left: A shepherdess in the Auvergne keeps busy while her goats feed.

The major cattle markets are at Agen (in the Lot et Garonne), Château Gontier (Mayenne), Fougères (Ille et Vilaine), Laissac (Aveyron), Parthenay (Deux Sèvres) and Sancoins (Cher).

Right: The market at Nasbinals where a dealer judges weight by touching the animal's rump.

Opposite:
Top left: Horse dealers – maquignons – in the Pays Basque.

Centre left: Cattle ready for auction at Sancoins in the Cher.

Below left: The annual market for pottioks (a kind of pony) which takes place each February in the Pays Basque.

Above right: A lively bar at a market near Moulins, north of Vichy.

France has twenty-four million head of cattle – more than any European country. Its pig population (twelve million) is the third largest, and its sheep flock (eleven million) the fourth largest, in Europe. Animal products account for over half the country's agricultural revenue and each year over four million cattle are sold at market.

The rustic atmosphere of the market continues and dealers enjoy heated bargaining, fuelled by a glass of wine, a swig of cider or a nip of marc, accompanied by bread with *pâté de campagne* or, in Brittany, a *galette-saucisse*. Until recently transactions were agreed verbally and conducted entirely in cash.

With the demise of horse-drawn equipment, true *maquignons* (horse dealers) are rare – the word has taken on a pejorative meaning – and horse markets have all but disappeared except in some of the more remote rural regions.

What better symbol of peace and contentment could there be than the fisherman? Sitting in his boat, or daydreaming among the reeds by an unpolluted river (there are still a few left), miles from the city, surrounded by iridescent dragonflies, he waits for hours on end to hook a fish that was happy enough itself until he finally came along.

In France they will eat any kind of river fish from the tiniest *ablette* to the largest salmon, and the aim of every country angler is the same – to bring home a prize for the family dinner table.

Freshwater fish soup cooked with a Burgundy wine and served with croûtons rubbed with garlic; grilled Loire salmon; shad from the river Garonne cooked with sorrel, using the roes in its stuffing; pike *quenelles* (a kind of dumpling) served with a velvety *nantua* sauce made with crayfish and fresh cream ... these are just a few of the innumerable delicious country recipes which require the basic ingredient of freshly-caught river fish.

Above: The river Marne near Rheims.

Right: Fishing on the Loire.

This curious form of hunting is practised only in south-west France, mainly in the Landes. It takes place in early autumn, when the wild pigeons begin their winter migration to Africa. The hunters trap the pigeons, attracting them to their fate using *aplans* or decoy birds. These are tamed pigeons caught the year before. Their heads covered with strange little bonnets, they are attached by their feet to perches which are then raised by a pulley system to the top of the tall trees, while the hunters lie in wait down below in well-equipped hides.

When a flight of pigeons comes by, the hunter pulls a string which sets the decoys calling and flapping their wings to attract the tired travellers and induce them to land. Nearby the hunters have prepared a flat, clean area, invitingly sprinkled with seed, where folded nets are concealed. More decoys are secured under wire mesh to lure their fellows down. When the wild pigeons land, the net springs over them. They are put into cages, and later transferred to aviaries. They can be eaten all the year round, mainly in *salmis* (partially roasted then prepared with a special sauce), but some will be kept alive to serve as next year's decoys. I was introduced to the sport by master chef, Michel Guérard.

Top left: A hooded decoy pigeon.

Above: Perch and decoy are raised by pulley.

Above: A camouflaged observation hut for the 'hunters'.

Left: Live, tamed pigeons act as decoys for their unsuspecting friends.

The French countryside is occasionally punctuated by an enchanting small tower sitting amidst a field of vines or sunflowers, some decorated with arches and topped by a spire or unusual weather-vane. They are pigeon coops, or dovecots, many of them architectural masterpieces.

A pigeon coop was once a fair indicator of the social standing of its owner as the building of a raised tower such as these was the privilege of feudal lords, and later limited to those owning more than fifty acres of land; everyone else had to make do with a small aviary. Usually a round tower belonged to a castle, a square tower to a family manor or farm. The particular styles shown here are peculiar to the area of southern France around Toulouse in the Haute Garonne.

126

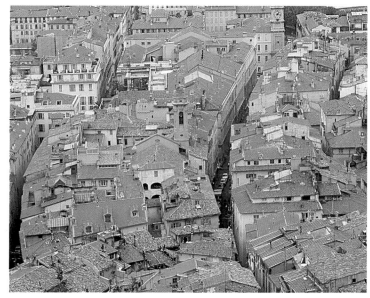

Throughout France, the roofs of all buildings, from châteaux and manoirs to the humblest cottages, are made of local materials, mineral or vegetable, and so they blend perfectly with their surroundings. Take, for example, the curved tiles of Provence, the slates of Anjou and Brittany, the Normandy thatch, the fish-scale patterns on roofs in Alsace.

The shape of the roofs varies depending on the climate of the region. North of the Loire you find steeply sloping roofs, making up two-thirds of the height of the house, which is how the Gauls used to build them. In the south, on the other hand, the legacy of the Romans is very flat roofs, representing at most a third of the height of the house. Details such as ridge tiling, cornices, dormer windows and chimney-stacks, all the features that support, give light to or decorate a roof, vary according to the area and the local materials. And so in France roofs constitute a sort of landscape within a landscape. Sadly, as elsewhere, this is gradually being disturbed by the advent of artificial materials and mass production. However, there is a reaction against this. Whole villages have been restored, and there are now institutes, both public and private, reviving traditional techniques.

Right: A farm building near Sarlat, Dordogne.

Opposite:
Above left: Sévérac le Château, Aveyron.

Centre left: Minerve in the Hérault.

Below left: Chinon on the Loire.

Above right: Nice on the Côte d'Azur.

Centre right: Ste Agnès near Menton.

Below right: Ségur le Château in the Limousin region.

129

In France, as everywhere, the advance of commercialization has had a serious effect on small shops, particularly food shops, tens of thousands of which have disappeared in the last twenty years. Even so, small, independent traders still exist, complementing the services of the large retailers. Often they can offer more choice and better quality, and if their prices are higher it seems only fair to pay a little more to feel at home and be served by a familiar face.

As a result, old shops still exist in villages and small towns, and even, tucked away, in the big cities. There is a growing trend among their owners to keep the original decor and features, retaining the character of the streets. The colours and signs look especially charming in these days of plastic and supermarkets.

Above left: A ladies' underwear shop in Vannes, Brittany.

Centre left: A small village bakery.

Below left: A grocery and hardware shop in the Aveyron region.

Above: A butcher's shop and charcuterie.

Right: A traditional tobacconist's at Cotignac, Provence.

130

Above: Awaiting the finish of a cycle race near Ste Maxime in the Côte d'Azur. Cycling and football are the two most popular sports in France.

Left: In Rémuzat, Provence, a Sunday game of belote, the bizarre card game rather like nap, which since the turn of the century has ousted the game of manille in café backrooms.

Above: A game of skittles, less popular now than boules but equally skilled.

Left: The game of 'baby-foot', or bar football on the seafront at Nice.

Below: An old man reads La Dépêche du Midi, his regional newspaper, at his window in Cordes.

Above right: Pausing for a conversation in St Félix de Lauragais, in the Haute Garonne.

Below right: In the same village, old friends watch the annual village fête.

Out in the villages it is still quite common, even today, to see old women dressed in the traditional black costume of mourning. You find it more as you travel further south towards the sunny Mediterranean.

It is well known that women generally stand up rather better than men to the hard life in the country. The fact that they also drink, or used to drink, less alcohol may have something to do with this. In any case, their life expectancy is still longer than men's. In times past, when they put on their widows' weeds it would be for the rest of their lives. Nor was it only widows who wore black. The whole family used to go into mourning when a relative died.

Left: Children visit their grandparents in the country.

Below: An old lady outside her house near Rochemenier, in Maine et Loire.

Even today there are still some old women who no longer bother to renew their wardrobe, but follow the dour custom. This may have something to do with the fact that they don't wash all that often, and that black is supposed not to show the dirt too much!

Here they are, in their villages, these grannies, with their long life of toil behind them. No longer strong enough to work in the fields, they sit on the doorstep with their knitting, exchanging the latest gossip, or feed grain to the chickens. Children love their company because they always have stories to tell, and a wealth of knowledge about the life and history of the village that they keep alive as younger people move away.

135

Most country people in France share one major form of relaxation: hunting. An enjoyable ritual during the season is the moment when the huntsmen, who have been up since before dawn, get together in the hunting lodge for a huge, late lunch. Everyone round the table is a gourmet and, after covering miles on foot, ravenous into the bargain. Usually prepared by the game-keeper's wife, the hunting lunch is a lavish meal consisting of simple but exceptionally delicious *cuisine bourgeoise*, washed down with plenty of wine, and is an important feature of good living in rural France.

The wood-burning stove is the heart of the farmhouse. An aromatic *daube* or *ragoût* simmers away on it, to be finished off in the *bain-marie*, a hot-water contraption on the right of the cooking plate. It is not far from the stove to the table, where the meal will be served up straight from the pan, after the men have drawn wine from a barrel in the cellar.

French provincial cooking is a fine art which has been handed down from generation to generation, and the visitor to the kitchen of Monsieur and Madame Gras is in the happy position of knowing he's going to eat well.

The time has long since passed when villages were self-sufficient and everyone had a particular skill to offer the community. However, there are still a few remnants of this forgotten age to be found in the form of local crafts.

Above left: Basket-weaving, for which the main material, osiers, grow widely in the Vendée, and for which there is a real demand.

Above: The clog-maker in Charité sur Loire is less fortunate; a few hippies did wear clogs in the 1970s, but nowadays he only makes them for the tourists, usually decorated with a place-name.

Below left: The Normandy farrier still gets a bit of work from people who have kept on their old carthorses for sentimental reasons. Farriers are often blacksmiths too, and some of them are presumably responsible for the ugly and pretentious ironwork you sometimes see on the second homes of people with more money than taste.

Right: The Provençal lady ironing a traditional head-dress comes into her own during religious festivals, when locals adopt national costume. The head-dress is nearly always made of white cotton lawn, and is stiffened with a starch (made of potato flour or rice water) which is 'cooked' by the hot iron. The intricate ruffles are made to stand out by using this special poker-shaped iron.

Above: Lace used to be counted as part of a family's wealth and was always included in a bride's trousseau. Today the lace industry has virtually disappeared, but in some regions, for example around Le Puy in the Auvergne where this elderly lady is working, it is still possible to see lacemakers working with bobbins in the traditional way. Some of these surviving lace-makers supply merchants who sell to the Arab nations – an original way for France to pay for its oil!

France's traditional festivals have been preserved in some parts of the country, and some quirky new ones are still being invented. The mayor of Bessières, a village in the major egg-producing area near Toulouse, has instituted the Festival of the Omelette on Easter Monday. Five and a half thousand eggs are broken into an enormous frying-pan. The eggs are beaten by machine, and three thousand portions of omelette are served to all comers, with bread provided by the local bakers.

On 24 and 25 May every year gypsies from all over Europe converge in pilgrimage on Stes Maries de la Mer, in the Bouches du Rhône. This is where, according to legend, Mary Jacobé, sister of the Virgin Mary, and Mary Salomé came ashore, after their expulsion from Judea, with their black servant Sarah, who became the patron saint of gypsies. On the second day, after much ceremony, the festival moves to the beach for the blessing of the sea.

In Béthune, in the Pas de Calais, the big day is 1 December, the festival of St Eloi, patron saint of goldsmiths and blacksmiths. He was adviser to Dagobert I, King of the Franks, and is immortalized in a children's song which recalls how one day King Dagobert put his trousers on the wrong way round, whereupon Eloi helpfully pointed this out and the King 'adjusted his dress'.

The festival of the May tree, in the Dordogne area, goes back to 1870, when elections used always to take place in May. It became the custom for candidates to plant a tree when they made their campaign speeches. Nowadays the ceremony of the May tree takes place at election-time, regardless of the time of year.

THE FOOD OF FRANCE

Cooking is an exhalted art in France. The international language of food is French, the standards set by its greatest chefs have always been recognised worldwide, and its culinary influence is unsurpassed. Haute cuisine, like haute couture, is the province of a tiny élite of rich and indulgent people, many of them foreigners, who seek the very best and are able to pay for it. To reach the top as a chef in France is to achieve a status similar to that accorded film stars elsewhere. Getting there is tremendously difficult: having first proved your genius in an art form that has strict codes and formidable technical exams, you also need the personality to match. Those who possess this powerful combination are likely to receive the highest accolades, some even being awarded the coveted Légion d'honneur.

We visitors arrive armed with our little red food bibles – the guidebooks whose rosettes indicate the culinary standing of chefs throughout the country, providing another incentive for the fierce competition between restaurants, routiers, cafés and brasseries. André Michelin compiled his first guide as long ago as 1900, so that from the dawn of motoring drivers knew where to buy petrol, get the car mended, sleep for the night and, of course, eat well anywhere in France.

Today, as ever, dramatic controversies and theatrical political infighting are prevalent among the small coterie of glamorous superstar chefs. They are called upon to endorse products only vaguely connected with their profession, and seem to sign and sell one of their cookbooks with every couvert, such is their international popularity. To say the French chef takes his profession seriously is a gross understatement, and always has been. Three centuries ago, the Prince de Condé's celebrated chef Vatel reacted to the news that the fish course was late at a dinner for the King by running himself through with a sword!

There is a great divide between restaurant cuisine and domestic cooking, but perfectionism is common to both. I have a vivid and pleasant memory of eating at the home of a wine-grower in Burgundy. The meal itself was very simple, but it was accompanied by the most delicious butter. When I asked my hostess where she had bought it, she told me it was from a farmer some twenty-five kilometers away – quite a journey for a pat of butter! In any village or town, everyone is an expert on the best place to shop for a particular item of food. Personal preference seems to have little to do with the strict pecking order – one charcuterie is the best for pâté, but another must be visited for ham. In Paris, people drive for miles to get the finest Camembert for Sunday lunch, and every day, usually twice a day, over the length and breadth of the country, at least one member of the family shops for fresh bread. The price of bread is still a national indicator of the cost of living.

The French have an honest approach to food which is reflected not only in the open pleasure with which they consume it, but also in their lack of squeamishness about how and from what those mouthwatering specialities are produced. The outsider often shudders when presented with tripe and other deliciously cooked offal, or frogs legs, snails, rabbit and horse meat. The French never give it a thought, and feel not a moment's guilt in force-feeding geese and duck for foie gras, or plunging a live trout into a boiling bouillon.

They were far more agitated about what went into hamburgers when fast-food chains invaded the land – and rightly so, though sadly these have now become established despite the early barrage of protest. The traditional French charcuterie and boulangerie have long catered for those who wish to buy ready-prepared food of high quality, and they have responded to the challenge of American-style fast food with the establishment of take-aways where exquisite dishes are the order of the day. Also, frozen versions of the great chefs' specialities are now mass-produced for those who can afford to reject fish fingers.

Filling the stomach still remains a fine art in France and a central part of the culture, despite a recent statistic that indicated that only fifty per cent of the population was now interested in food. Nowhere else on earth could such a statement be made – and be so patently untrue!

The archetypal caricature of a Frenchman shows him wearing a beret, with a *baguette* tucked under his arm. You may have to look hard nowadays to find a real Frenchman in a beret, but, as mealtimes approach, you still see just as many *baguettes* under people's arms or protruding from shopping-bags.

However, the French consumption of bread has declined. It has fallen from three hundred kilos per head per year in the last century to less than sixty kilos today, and by fifty per cent just since the last war. The reason is that, even though bread is still the best value food available, there is less poverty today, so people are no longer so reliant on it as a staple diet. In the old days an increase in the price of bread caused rioting. In the early days of the Revolution the mob marching on Versailles was not after the king, the queen and the little prince, but after the baker, the baker's wife and the baker's son. . . .

A couple of decades ago bread came under attack from dieticians. It was accused of being fattening and difficult to digest. But medical opinions tend to change like fashions, and today most dieticians agree that bread is not fattening as long as you eat it in moderation.

Now it is the consumers who complain: bread is not what it used to be, it is tasteless, it goes stale too quickly, the crust is soggy. . . . In fact the baking of bread is still almost exclusively a cottage industry in France, and if the baker is good at his job, then the bread will be good. Every area has its local bakeries, and to find the best all you have to do is watch and see where the queues form when a fresh batch is ready.

The ancestry of today's bread-loving Frenchman goes back a long way, but the history of bread goes back even further. The baker's familiar gesture as he slides the dough into the oven is as old as that of the sower casting seeds, and is depicted in the frescoes which decorate the

144

Pharaohs' tombs. Rome under Augustus was blessed with no fewer than three hundred baker's shops. Most of them were run by Greeks, who often had Gauls as assistants – an early pointer, perhaps, to the later French passion for bread.

The symbolic significance of bread, like that of wine, has been much enhanced by the Christian tradition. It is still referred to as the 'staff of life', and until quite recently it was still common in some French families to cut a cross in the top of a loaf of bread before breaking it. A certain amount of superstition grew up around it too: many people still think it's bad luck to see a loaf of bread placed upside down.

There are many expressions in the French language, some very similar to English ones, that testify to the perennial importance of bread as the symbol of life: *gagner son pain*, meaning to earn one's living; *avoir du pain sur la planche*, to have a lot on one's plate; and a new expression, much used by the young, *ça ne mange pas de pain*, meaning it won't cost anything, or you're not committing yourself to anything.

Opposite:
Above: The early-morning visit to the boulangerie, is one of the French rituals.

Below: For a village without a bakery, fresh bread arrives twice-daily by van.

This page:
Left: The reward for fetching fresh bread for breakfast.

Above: A meal without bread is unthinkable to the French.

Scenes inside the bakehouse, where the baker goes to work at the crack of dawn – and sometimes works all through the night – to produce the early morning batch of bread: it is here that the three processes of kneading, fermenting and baking take place. The key to really good bread is good kneading, an art in itself and as crucial as using the right flour. Today most bakers use electric ovens, but some have gone back to using wood-fired ovens to produce bread the old-fashioned way.

The French have several ways of testing to see if a loaf is good: it should feel quite heavy for its size; tapping it with a finger should produce a resonant sound; the crust should be quite thick, very crisp and golden, and should not come apart when you press it; the crumb should not be too white and should have a waxy, elastic texture; and it is better that a loaf smells very slightly acid. Two cardinal rules with French bread are: never cut or break a loaf more than ten minutes before serving it, and never keep bread in a plastic bag – the best way to store it is in a paper bag, a wooden box, or wrapped in a napkin.

Top: Kneading the dough.

Above: Preparing to bake.

Left: A stock of uncooked dough.

Left: Cake bases in the oven.

Below: Lionel Poilâne, master baker, in the back of his shop, Poilâne, in Paris.

147

As well as producing unbeatable bread, French bakers also service the nation's sweet tooth with a cornucopia of pastries and cakes. One of the most enjoyable French customs is the visit to the *boulangerie-pâtisserie* after Mass on Sundays – whether you attended the service or not! – returning home with a baguette in one hand and a pyramid-shaped parcel in the other, containing a shining *tarte aux fruits* or a *mille feuille* heavy with *crème pâtissière*.

Top left: A mouth-watering display of pâtisserie at Sarlat, in Périgord.

Centre left: The exterior of Poilâne in Paris. Lionel Poilâne is famous throughout France for having revived the art of making bread the traditional way.

Below left: A Parisian curiosity. At this boulangerie in Boulevard Haussmann, the baker carries on the ancient tradition of sculpting in dough.

Below: This Parisian charmer entices customers into a shop in Faubourg St Martin.

Right: A boulanger-patissier in Paris, who is not only a master of his craft, but was obviously predestined to be so, for his name is Marcel Pain.

Whether ornately packaged in a sophisticated Parisian emporium or presented quite simply in a country market, French pastries and confectionary are unbeatable.

Above: In the Landes this woman sells jams and preserves made with fruit from her own garden.

Top: A spectacular counter of sweets and jams at Hédiard in Paris.

Left: An austere array of rich homemade tarts in Périgueux.

Food shops are probably more numerous and play a more important social role in French towns and villages than anywhere else in the world. It is not unusual for a tiny village to boast two butchers and two bakers, in which case it is up to the customers to spread their favours evenly to avoid causing resentment, or at least to drop in occasionally for a token purchase at the less favoured shop in order to keep on good terms with everyone. You never know when you might need a favour. Even in the big cities the advent of supermarkets has not done away with the small local shops, and in residential areas there are still specific streets of little shops which supply the locals with their food; in fact the very best shops are often found in these areas.

Buying food (*la bouffe*, as they call it these days) is a spontaneous, pleasurable activity for the French, which each person approaches in his or her own particular way. A housewife on a restricted budget will be especially hard to please: she wants value for money and knows how to get it. She is probably a good cook, and skilled at selecting food for its freshness and choosing cheese at just the right degree of ripeness. Occasionally she will splash out on something special like oysters, *pâté de foie gras* or asparagus (the first of the season, of course), well aware she will have to compensate her budget

Right: The interior of the Boucherie Lamartine.

Below: The Boucherie Lamartine, one of the best butcher's shops in Paris.

Bottom: The decorative façade of the Chiapello grocery in the flower market in Nice.

by cutting back on clothes or outings. She, like all regular customers, will probably want to build up a rapport with the shopkeeper to ensure she gets good service.

Modest or luxurious, every type of shop has its own character and often its own particular colour scheme. Butcher's, horse butcher's and tripe shops always used to be red, the colour of ox blood (*sang de boeuf*), but are sometimes now a deeper, claret colour which looks rather more distinguished. Dairy shops go in for fresher colours, the background often a creamy white, halfway between milk and butter, with little touches of blue and green. Many feature the figure of a cow in a field, either behind glass or as a mosaic, and have cool, white marble counters. Fishmongers use the colours of the sea, green, silver-grey and deep blue, while greengrocers fall back on the simple device of painting their wooden stalls a good rustic green, suggesting the kitchen garden. Grocers have more freedom, usually relying on lavish packaging, wooden shelving and copper hanging rails, and sometimes putting huge glass jars full of attractively coloured sweets and delicacies outside on the pavement. All these traditions change over the years, but it is remarkable how many traces of them still remain, particularly in the most sophisticated areas.

153

Above: In addition to pork products, most charcuteries stock jams, preserves and vegetable dishes like grated carrot.

Right: Meat being smoked at Orchamps-Vennes, in the Doubs. The process takes three or four weeks.

As we know from the famous *Astérix* books, the ancient Gauls used to hunt wild boar (*sanglier*) in the forests, and would feast on the roasted meat, washing it down with *cervoise*, or barley beer. The wild boar was later replaced by the pig on the tables of the Gallo-Romans, the Franks and finally the French. A close relative of the boar, the pig was also a wild animal originally, and fed on acorns. Today it provides a source of heavy, rich, but relatively inexpensive food.

'Tout est bon dans le cochon' – everything in the pig is good to eat, goes the old saying. The result is the amazing number of *cochonailles*, or pork products, of which every region of France claims to have its own speciality: hams, cooked or raw, salted or smoked, *jambonneau* (knuckle of ham), sausages and *saucissons, pieds de porc* (trotters), black pudding, *rillettes* (potted meats), *andouilles* (chitterling sausages), their

smaller sisters, *andouillettes*, and *cervelas* (saveloy). In addition there is a vast range of pork pâtés and terrines.

In many country areas pig-killing has always been and still is one of the major events of the year. People used to prepare for it well in advance, gathering all the family together and extracting from the animal enough food to keep themselves going for months. The timing of the ceremony varied from region to region. Usually it was done on Shrove Tuesday, so that the meat could be taken out of the salting tub at Easter-time, but sometimes it was done earlier, towards the end of January, for the feast of St Anthony, patron saint of pork butchers.

Above: Pâtés and rillettes.

Top: A charcuterie stall in Périgord, with saucissons made from pork.

155

Some provincial towns hold their main markets indoors. A great covered market like this one at Villefranche sur Saône (*left*), a small industrial and commercial town north of Lyons in the Beaujolais district, is a busy meeting-place for housewives and provides an important part of their social life. The district councils are generally very keen to preserve this kind of building, which usually stands in the middle of a square, in the centre of town. Sometimes it is a splendid old granary, restored and converted for use as a market; sometimes, unfortunately, it is a concrete monstrosity in the 'aircraft hangar' style which some architects went in for during the 1950s – though, to be fair, they did meet the most important criteria of reconstruction in that post-war period which were speed and ease of manufacture. Still, they serve their purpose, and in rainy areas having a roof over one's head is a blessing. As in open-air markets, you are soon caught up in the excitement of seeing so much fresh, local produce being sold with such speed and energy. The produce has all come straight here from an assembly point just outside the town, where, as soon as dawn breaks, streams of vehicles – lorries, vans, cars with boots filled to the brim, even wheelbarrows – converge, laden with mountains of fruit and vegetables from huge farms and tiny kitchen gardens.

Anything superfluous to local demand goes straight off to Rungis (*above*). This vast market, the stomach of Paris, has literally everything needed to satisfy the gastronomic demands of the capital – and there is no more demanding city in the world. Whatever you want, from *chanterelles*, gathered wild from French forests, to frozen Korean crayfish, can be found here, and there is a superb, breathtaking flower market. But sadly, despite its undoubted efficiency, Rungis has none of the charm and excitement of the old market in Les Halles in central Paris.

There is no more cheerful way of watching the seasons revolve than to observe the open-air markets. Here the coming of spring is heralded by the arrival of the new young vegetables. Carrots, for example, which were sold loose during the winter, now suddenly appear in neat bunches, with elegant green feathers of leaves smelling faintly of aniseed – a sure sign of freshness. Tender lettuces are arranged in small piles. Tomatoes by the crateful bask in the sun. Small artichokes are sold in bouquets, and mauve and white asparagus in bunches, to protect the delicate tips. Equally appetizing are the onions, peas, beans and the new potatoes, shiny and golden. Then comes the fruit, in profusion – mountains of strawberries, pyramids of melons. If you want to save money, come late in the day, when the vendors lower their prices.

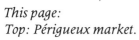

This page:
Top: Périgueux market.

Above: A discriminating customer – they are not all women – feels the melons for ripeness.

Right: Inspection of pigeons at the poultry market at Toulouse.

Opposite:
Top: A profusion of fruit and vegetables at a greengrocer's stall.

Below left: In the countryside, poultry is sold live and the customer is expected to know how to deal with it.

Below right: A tempting display of olives and pickles in Sarlat market.

In the market at Limoux, near Carcassonne, a philosophical garlic seller sits with his mountain of cloves, patiently waiting for customers. He might well be the best source of tips on how to use the miraculous clove, queen of Provençal cuisine: how, for example, to avoid indigestion, you remove the green germ in the middle; to make peeling easier, you plunge the garlic into hot water for a minute; and to clear your breath of the powerful smell of garlic, you eat a couple of sugar-lumps or a sprig of parsley after the meal.

A simple table, laid almost as for a family meal, is typical of the way cheese is sold in a small open-air market. Only one kind of cheese is offered, but it is local, farmhouse cheese, made with milk straight from the cow, goat or ewe. Rustic-looking in shape and colour, cheese like this is superb in the springtime, when it tastes of the young, tender grass on which the animals have been grazing. It will have been kept in a cool place but not refrigerated, won't have travelled far, and will be perfect for eating.

The delicate art of Camembert-making. Camembert was invented in 1791 by a Normandy farmer's wife called Marie Harel, and its famous wooden box in 1881 by the engineer Ridel.

Pyrenean cheeses, from Iraty in the Pays Basque. Made from raw pressed curds, with a natural, smooth crust, and matured in damp cellars, they are best eaten in the autumn.

Langoustines and crevettes at Quimper market in Brittany. They are sold alive and wriggling, then plunged, still alive, into a pan of boiling water, preferably strongly flavoured sea-water.

Straining the cheese. This is a crucial process which must be done very carefully, with the milk and the air at the right temperature, for perfect results.

Garden snails from the Poitou/Charente area. These unfortunates are put into a bucket to fast, where they froth away until they are roasted and eaten in their shells with butter and garlic.

The oyster-opener at the famous Parisian restaurant, Charlot. He has both the rounded kind, like Fines de Claires, and the more expensive, flat Belon and Marennes varieties.

Morels (morilles), an exceptional kind of mushroom. In springtime anyone can just go out and pick them and sell them at market. Morilles are superb in a creamy sauce with poultry.

The truffle market at Sarlat, Périgord. Truffles are 'hunted' in winter by dogs and pigs specially trained from birth to sniff them out. This is achieved by rubbing a truffle over the mothers' teats.

Some oyster-sellers will let you sample their wares before buying. The real cognoscenti eat them alive, quite plain, straight from the shell, with brown bread and butter and a dry white wine.

Another very popular kind of mushroom is the cèpe. The cap should be firm, with a thin skin, and the stalk full, tender and bright – a delight.

The force-feeding of geese or ducks. A mash of grains is forced into their stomachs; their livers grow fatter and fatter. The result is foie gras, sometimes flavoured with truffles.

Pure olive oil from Provence is sold under a variety of intimidating appellations: 'pure virgin', 'extra virgin', 'cold-pressed virgin', etc. – the certification proudly displayed.

LE KILOGRAMME

LE KILOGRAMME

'A country that produces over three hundred and fifty different cheeses is not easy to govern,' General de Gaulle once said (though some people claim it was Winston Churchill). In fact there are over four hundred different cheeses in France, which is the world's leading cheese producer, making over a million tons of it every year. Hard luck on successive governments, but good news for those who believe that a meal without cheese is like a bed without a pillow.

It is worth noting that there are two quite distinct kinds of cheese on the market today: farm cheeses, made with unpasteurized milk straight from the cow, goat or ewe, and pasteurized ones, which are becoming increasingly common since they can be made by industrial methods and stay consistent all the year — consistently bland, that is.

Real cheeses should be eaten in their proper seasons: fresh ewes' milk cheeses and Vacherin during the winter and spring; soft goat cheese, blue-veined cheese, Fourme, Roquefort and Tomme in spring and summer; soft cheeses made from fermented cows' milk — Brie, Camembert, Livarot — in autumn, winter and spring. Camembert is sold under about two thousand different brand names (of which five hundred are Normandy makes), but the very best comes from the Pays d'Auge.

Cheese comes in all shapes and sizes and, like bread and wine, has been around since the dawn of time. Charlemagne, it is said, was very partial to Brie and Roquefort, and at the time of the Revolution it was reckoned that the French ate three kilos of cheese per head every year.

Opinions vary as to whether cheese should be eaten before or after the dessert, but there is no argument about the fact that it is delicious with wine. Red wine is the best, though some recommend a dry white wine with goat cheese and Sauternes with Roquefort.

Cheese stall in Bordeaux.

We tend to think of France as a country where they live out of doors all the time, eating and drinking regally, and dancing in the streets in the evenings, as if every day were a holiday. The country festivals do have a particular charm, with the traditional bowls of cider, glasses of red wine and, nowadays, paper cones full of chips; and it is true that at the first hint of sun the café terraces fill up. However, while France is blessed with a temperate climate, some parts suffer very severe winter weather,

and the French themselves refer to something enjoyable that cannot last as being like *un déjeuner au soleil* – a meal in the sunshine.

Right: A huge, open-air meal under the trees in a village near Perpignan, one of the sunniest towns in the country. Foreigners tend to think that meals like this go on all the time, but here they are in fact celebrating the Fête Nationale.

Above: For services rendered ... A peasant shares his picnic with his dog at St Félix de Lauragais, in Aquitaine.

166

This vision of France as a land of colours and light owes much to the work of the Impressionists. At the time, paintings like Manet's *Déjeuner sur l'Herbe* (1862), which showed ordinary people enjoying themselves in the open air, caused quite a stir. These revolutionaries of the art world helped to create a revolution in people's lifestyles too. Until the late nineteenth century people mostly stayed at home – the poor because they could not afford to go out, the middle classes because it was

not the done thing. You simply did not go to a restaurant except on very special occasions. Then came the cheerful Belle Epoque and the 'mad years' after the First World War – party time had arrived, and the world had changed for the better.

Left: Another open-air meal, this time near Autun, a beautiful city in Burgundy on the edge of Morvan.

Above: A couple enjoying a simple picnic by the fountain in front of the Centre Pompidou in Paris.

Le Grand Véfour (*left*) is one of those temples of Parisian cuisine which have become rather more than just restaurants — more like historic monuments. Its fabulous Directoire decor (*centre right*) brings to mind the wild period just after the Revolution. For many years Véfour (which had not yet become Le Grand Véfour) had a rival under the arcades of the Palais Royal. This was Very, another famous restaurant, now gone, where the novelist Balzac claimed to have single-handedly demolished, in one evening in 1826, a hundred oysters, twelve cutlets, a duckling, two partridges and a sole!

Lucas Carton (*below*), in a corner of Place de la Madeleine, has splendid wood panelling from the school of Majorelle and seats upholstered in tobacco-coloured velvet. It used to be one of the most glittering venues of the Belle Epoque, when *demimondaines* had assignations in its intimate first-floor salons with monocled, moustachioed gentlemen in top hats. For a long time Marcel Proust lived just near here, in Boulevard Malesherbes. Alain Senderens, one of the kings of *nouvelle cuisine*, has revitalized this ancient, luxurious restaurant, but its prices ensure

that it is mainly used now by businessmen and Japanese tourists.

The Brasserie Lipp (*left*), in St Germain des Prés, is another fine example of Belle Epoque decor, and justly famous for its ceramics. You can't book a table here, so you just have to queue up, like everyone else — unless you happen to be famous yourself. But it's well worth it, not so much for the menu as for the people. It is like an annexe both of the Assemblée Nationale and of the great newspaper houses, which are all just around the corner.

Left: Le Grand Comptoir is a very different kind of establishment. One of the few survivals of the old Les Halles area, it consists of a simple café-tabac, leading to a huge room where you can eat good, old-fashioned food.

When Michel Oliver left Le Grand Véfour, Jean-Paul Bonin, former master chef at the Hôtel Crillon, was invited to succeed him and create the new menu. The task of producing this sumptuous menu fell to his assistant, André Signoret, who finally took control of everything and was so successful that he is now the titular head of this renowned restaurant. His menu includes, among other delicious things, *parmentier d'agneau*, a small joint of lamb roasted in a potato casing, fried *riz de veau* (calf sweetbread) and kidneys with lemon juice, and *tournedos Rossini* (medallions of fillet of beef), cooked to the exact Belle Epoque recipe.

Here at Pharamond the turn-of-the-century decor is pleasantly cosy, the walls covered in tiles decorated with flowers and fruit. It is all very appetizing, as you sit comfortably anticipating the delights of Alain Hyvonnet's splendid Normandy cooking. The highlight of the menu is this tripe dish, for which the place has been famous for decades. It is best accompanied by an excellent Auge cider or a fruity perry from Domfront. If you are not keen on tripe (it is an acquired taste), there are plenty of other first-class things from which to choose, for example, oysters and mussels *au beurre blanc*, or *la canette au citron* (duckling cooked with lemon).

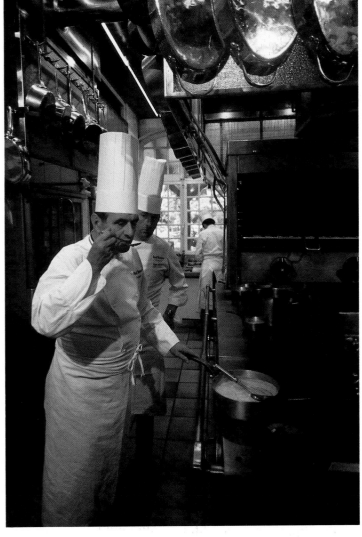

On the Côte Vermeille, at Collioure, is Yves Costa's restaurant, La Frégate, where you can taste sea-food cooked in every conceivable way. Yves Costa, seen here fortifying a speciality, was one of the first people in France to serve raw fish, in a dish called *tartare de la marée du jour* (mixed fresh fish from today's tide). In summer, out on the terrace, his customers can also enjoy *panachée de poissons en vessie* (mixed fish cooked in a bladder), fried lobster with herbs, *coquilles St Jacques* with chicory and pasta, with a 'green' wine sauce, or a *terrine de ratatouille aux anchois de Collioure* (ratatouille terrine with Collioure anchovies).

Paul Bocuse, seen here at his restaurant near Lyons sampling the work of a colleague, is a great man who has done much to make French cooking internationally popular again, through his generosity and his genius. Master of *nouvelle cuisine*, he is also a dab hand, when the need arises, at the great regional dishes like *navarin* (lamb ragout), or *gratin de cardons à la moëlle* (gratinéed cardoons with marrow). Moreover, from his kitchens emerge not only wonderfully inventive dishes but also a plethora of young cooks trained by him – he is essentially a teacher. After all, cooking is one of those arts handed down from one generation to the next.

At the turn of the century, there was Maxim's. And Maxim's is still there, the same as ever, with its *Omnibus*, its *Grande Salle* and little salons, its fancy curtains and red plush seats, where you can imagine La Belle Otéro stretching out a gloved hand to the Baron de Charlus. Most of the international jet set have been to Maxim's, but to average French people, it is just an impossible dream. For them it will be the familiar local restaurant, with a name, if it is in the provinces, like 'La Poste', 'Le Cheval Blanc', 'Le Lion d'Or' or 'Le Bon Coin', or if it is in Paris, 'La Devinière' or 'Chez Benoit'. Here, even in this dismal age of fast food and high-camp *nouvelle cuisine*, you can still find good unpretentious traditional cooking.

A revealing characteristic of the French is that whereas in most countries people like to eat with romantic, dimmed lighting, in France they like the lights full on – so they can get a good look at what they are eating.

Above left: Maxim's.

Below left: La Devinière, a Parisian 'local'.

Above: A simple Boulogne restaurant.

Right: Benoit's hilarious menu from the 1970s.

A long table, a bottle of wine, and a glass kept well topped up. Some may go for fine vintage wine, others for cheap, rough red, but all good Frenchmen, rich or poor, love their wine and mistrust those who drink only water.

France not only leads the world in both the production of wine and its consumption per head, it can also boast the finest wines. The French, of course, cannot claim to have invented the art of wine-making, though the ancient Gauls did make a major contribution: the barrel.

No one knows exactly when wine was first drunk, but it seems to have been around at the time of the Flood, since Noah is said to have been glad of a drink of wine on disembarking from the Ark. One can hardly blame him, after all those weeks on water!

Wine, like bread, is full of symbolism. The Greeks paid due respect to their god of wine, Dionysos, son of Zeus, and the Romans had an equivalent in Bacchus. It seems to have been consumed by all and sundry, and played a major part in all those Roman orgies described by historians from Pliny to Suetonius. Yet in ancient Rome it was strictly forbidden for women to drink wine. Cato the Elder, also known as the Censor, the one who went on about destroying Carthage, offered the following advice: 'If you catch your wife drinking wine, kill her!' History does not record whether he was a wine drinker himself.

In Christian times, the need for communion wine led to the monasteries playing an important role in the development of viticulture. According to Petrarch, Urban V, Pope of Avignon, took some persuading to return to Rome as he was very reluctant to leave behind his Clos de Vougeot vineyards.

A working men's lunch at Larceveau in the Pays Basque.

The most important time of year for the wine-maker is the early autumn, when all hands are called in to help with the *vendange*. Family and cousins rally round, working alongside students and young people from all walks of life. There are tons of grapes to be picked, bunch by bunch, and gathered together in huge baskets — and it is hard work.

The grape harvest is always a time for celebration, wherever it may be, and whatever kind of year it has been, for it is the culmination of months of work. The wine-maker knows already whether this year's wine will be good or poor, for the weather plays a crucial role in wine-growing. Success varies from place to place, according to the conditions. Here are a few examples: for Bordeaux, 1985 and 1982 are excellent years, or rather *will* be, as this is a wine which should not be drunk too young, and other good years are 1978, 1975, 1970 and 1961. For Burgundy, 1978 is *the* year, though 1976, 1971, 1966 and 1961 are also good. Beaujolais, Côtes du Rhône and particularly Alsatian wines were all exceptionally good in 1983.

Oenology, or the study of wines, has a charming vocabulary all of its own. A wine can be ample, harmonious, vigorous, gulpable, supple or virile; it has, one hopes, bouquet and body, while the French speak not of its colour but of its dress (*sa robe*).

Wine is produced all over France, in Burgundy and the Bordelais, Alsace and Champagne, the Loire, the Rhône, Provence and Languedoc, not to mention all the intermediate regions (such as the whole of Aquitaine). In fact it is only in the far north and at altitudes of over three hundred metres, where vines will not grow, that it is not produced.

Cultivation of the vine was introduced to France by the Romans, and within decades it had spread all over the country, even to areas where the invaders never dreamed it could be successfully grown. Before long the Romans began to grow alarmed that their enthusiastic neighbours were altogether too successful and posing a threat to their own vineyards, and in AD 91 the Emperor Domitian ordered half the vines in Gaul to be uprooted. Luckily this order was not properly carried out, and was rescinded by a subsequent emperor.

In those days there were vineyards in places where they have long since disappeared. A few centuries ago wine was being produced in Paris at Montmartre, St Denis and St Germain. It was probably awful, gut-rotting stuff, but at least it was better than the local water, which in those days was dreadfully polluted. The wine from Montmartre and the surrounding area was known as *guinguet* and was the usual tipple in the little places of entertainment along the banks of the Seine which later became known as *guinguettes*.

Top left: Pruning the vines at Fort de Salses in Roussillon.

Centre left: A well-kept vineyard near Soulignac, south of Limoges.

Below left: The Beaujolais grape harvest.

Right: A fine vintage? The wine-maker already has a pretty good idea.

After picking, the grapes are crushed. In the old days, they were trampled by foot, an operation which often turned into a dance, accompanied by much singing. Today it is all done by machine. When black grapes have been crushed, the resulting 'must' (*moûts*) will produce red wine if the skins are left in, and white wine if it is now pressed and the skins removed. White grapes, of course, always produce white wine. The must is then put into huge open tubs, made of wood, cement or brick, to ferment. This can go on for days or weeks. Sometimes a little sugar is added, in a process known as chaptalization (after the famous physician who invented it). This is strictly controlled by law, as it increases the wine's alcohol content and can also spoil it if not carefully regulated.

The tubs have to be kept topped up to prevent the formation of a mould known as the 'flowers' of a wine. Then, after the *marc* has been separated off for distillation, the wine is put into barrels, or straight into bottles, where it will age.

Nowadays everyone knows that wine ages best in a cellar, but this was only discovered quite by chance. The Romans used to keep their wine in amphorae, and it was the medieval monks who first put wine in their cellars – not to improve it, but to hide it from pillagers and avoid showing their gluttony.

Top left and right: Harvesting in Burgundy and the Dordogne.

Centre: Above the picturesque Alsatian town of Riquewihr, the grapes are carted away to the crushing machine.

Below left: A cave, or cellar, in Touraine.

Below right: The excellent wine cellar of the Intercontinental Hotel in Paris.

Opposite: Wine presses at a Beaujolais co-operative.

Now to the very best: champagne. By law, champagne must come from Champagne alone – an area of vineyards, 85,000 acres in size. It is the glorious pinnacle of France's wine industry. Annual sales are not far below 20 million bottles a year worldwide, enormously helped by the vast amount consumed in Britain and America. A marketing genius could not have dreamed up a better history for this superb wine, or created a more desirable, glamorous and luxurious image. In the ancient capital of the region, Rheims, when medieval kings were crowned they were toasted with a wine, originally from Ay in the Marne, which had a pleasing sparkle. It was grey (*gris*) and intoxicating (*grisant*), highly popular with the courts of France and England by the 1600s, and extremely rare. The brilliant cellarer-monk, Dom Pérignon, by the time he died in 1715, had perfected a method of creating and preserving the carbonic gas in the wine, and of producing quantities of champagne. In true French style, it was given pride of place, recognized as the finest of wines for only the finest occasions. The popping of champagne corks became synonymous with celebration.

Above left: At Hautvilliers, where Dom Pérignon perfected champagne, a bottle is ceremoniously opened by sword.

Above: A wedding at Cahors in south-west France.

Right: Champagne caves in Rheims.

a maison

THE FRENCH HOME

When French houses aren't overblown, like the flamboyant châteaux of the Loire valley, they're remarkably simple. For the most part, villas and town houses have plain façades relieved by shutters, handsome windows and doors. This subtle plainness gives them a wonderfully graphic quality that also makes them quite timeless, whatever their particular architectural style. But they have other charms too. In small towns and throughout the south, houses are rendered or washed in bright, pigmented colours – reds predominate in a profusion of shades, but you'll also find blues, yellows and ochre. As these fade in the dazzling sun they develop a lovely patina that gives them a painterly quality, raising them from sometimes quite humdrum buildings to objects of pleasing decay. So no matter how plain, French houses are far more appealing than a basic architectural description would make you believe.

There is a rich variation of architectural styles in France, not so much because of any great change in plan or building type, but because materials differ so widely. In Alsace, the houses seem very German. They are not really, but their half-timbered style reflects the buildings of northern and central Europe. Elsewhere in France, brick is widely used, and in some areas, including Paris, the townscape is in a beautiful honey-coloured stone with wonderful grey slate roofs. In southern France, houses are built quite simply of clay – a beautiful and surprisingly practical material. In Picardy, the houses are sculpted from clay and then simply rendered. In the Caux region of Normandy, mud walls are indented with pebbles, shingle and flint. In the Soissonnais and Valois regions, stone predominates – often with fine-cut ashlar finishes. In Argonne and throughout the Alps, timber is the mainstay of the building industry. Along the Mediterranean, roofs are often flat; in the Basque country the vast overhanging eaves of steep-pitched roofs nearly touch the ground. The variety seems endless. When you contrast mud houses in the Basque country with fine urban compositions like Place des Vosges in Paris, you become very aware of the dichotomy between urban and rural ways of life.

Interestingly, interiors are often at their best when taken to the extremes of urban or rural styles. There's something particularly dreary about the average French small-town interior – fusty, rigid, too correct for comfort – but something definitely appealing about a country kitchen or parlour, or an ultra-modern city interior like Philippe Starck's private apartments for President Mitterrand at the Elysée Palace.

Another appealing feature of country living is the extended dining room, spilling out into the courtyard or garden, inviting the occupants to step into the fresh air for a long, delicious lunch in the shade. The French have a greater passion and need for garden furniture than almost any other nation, and they take it as seriously as the English do their three-piece suite.

In many of the best interiors, whether in town or country, there is a certain starkness in design based on the influence of rural peasant homes and Mediterranean simplicity. As a result, objects like cooking utensils, crockery and cutlery, simple vases and modern lamps, textile covers and paintings on the wall, assume an important part of the decoration.

This habit of making a virtue of the functional is again reflected in the façades of houses. It is still rare to come across the kind of stick-on, decorative clutter in French towns that you find constantly in Britain. The houses are allowed to speak for themselves, and it is the essential details like the shutters, surface materials and roofs, that give French houses their character.

So although often out-of-date and sometimes a little dry, the average French home inside and out is a lot less phoney than its English counterpart. It is this honest, earthy quality that makes living, particularly rural living, in France such a joy. In any case, French people seem to know instinctively that the house per se isn't the most important thing – it's the cooking, wining, dining, loving, gossip and play that go on inside that really matters, and for those reasons alone a simple stage is often the best.

For the most part French entrances are as elegant as the manners of the people they were designed for and, in many cases, those who now live behind them.

Although formal, the linear avenue is still welcoming. A mature avenue of plane trees in St Rémy de Provence (*above left*) is beautiful in itself. Near Arles, open country gates (*below left*) entice the visitor along the shady, chestnut-tree-lined walk to the handsome house filling the vista at the end of the avenue. The trees were planted here to protect farm workers and animals from the burning sun as they made their way to and from the fields. The gulleys running on either side of the avenue were dug to provide flowing water for their refreshment. The total effect, if alien to the English mind with its preference for cosy twisting lanes, is rational, commonsensical and humane, which just about sums up a good deal of the French attitude towards design, if not always towards architecture.

When the French decide to be distant and mysterious they secure their houses behind formidable locked gates. No matter how attractive, the pointed, spiked and well-secured gate (*right*), in the Languedoc, tells visitors in no uncertain terms to 'keep out'. The French are obsessed with security, perhaps not surprisingly in a country of tense political dramas. So, increasingly, gates like these are topped with swivelling security cameras and remote-control locking mechanisms.

Life in the French town house is guarded from public view behind cliffs of plain walls, tight-fitting, tall gates and fearsome concierges. Children playing, a splashing fountain, women in conversation, are caught momentarily by the wandering visitor, catching a glimpse through to the all-important courtyard. In Old Nice (*below right*) the busy atmosphere is reminiscent of Italy. In contrast, a tapestry-like garden (*opposite*) hides behind the creamy pink blocks and austere gates of the façade of an elegant building in the Place des Vosges in Paris, once a royal residence.

An exuberant apartment block (*above left*) by Lavirotte, *c.*1900, is equally private. Art Nouveau swirls form a crusty carapace protecting the interior privacy, and despite balcony views out, you can't possibly see in from the street. In the country, houses need not hide. The fashion set by the Petit Trianon at Versailles for freestanding classical pavilions is seen in this eighteenth-century villa near Aix-en-Provence (*above right*). In Alsace one finds wonderfully homely structures like this one in Hunawihr (*below left*), characterized by its timber frame and fish-scale tiles.

The variations in geography, natural resources, climate, heritage and culture, have produced a rich patchwork of patterns and textures on buildings.

Opposite:
Top left: The sun plays on a rough stone barn in Clos Ste Mère.

Top right: A precision-made stone wall decorated with superimposed pebbles, in Aujan Mournède.

Centre left: Hard, dark limestone set into softer stone forms a Romanesque frieze on the twelfth-century church of St Austremoine in the Auvergne.

Centre right: Brick, sandstone and flint decorate the walls of a pigeon house in Normandy.

Below left: Artificially buckled and naturally rusted, corrugated iron has a pleasing rural decay that blends into natural settings despite its industrial heritage. This barn is in the Ile de France.

Below right: A sundial is set into the brickwork of the abbey church at Moissac in Tarn et Garonne.

This page:
Above: A criss-cross timber-framed house in Auch; the wealthy had the frames filled with brick, while the poor made do with clay, or wattle and daub.

Below: A delicate herring-bone of tiles stitched into the walls of a Normandy farmhouse.

The farmhouses in France often have two doors – one tall and narrow, for the human occupants, and one low and broad-shouldered, for the animals. Traditionally animals and owners lived in a high-smelling huddle under the same roof.

The colours of doors are often stunning, particularly when finished to a high-glossed perfection as only French painters seem able to achieve, but equally pleasing when bleached for years by the sun into a wash-like patina.

Opposite: A superb façade with paintwork like a faded fabric, belonging to a farmhouse near Beaujeu in the Beaujolais country.

This page:
Above left: a classic farmhouse door in Berstett, near Strasbourg, is painted in a turquoise, common throughout France, which acts as a fly repellent!

Above right: Patterned doors abound – some geometrical, others more florid like this town house in Provence.

Below left: A beautiful Art Deco door in rue Mallet-Stevens in Paris.

Below right: In town, doors are more formal, often classically proportioned, and painted a deep, bottle green that reads almost black, but without black's severe grandeur. This paint never seems to fade and is as shiny as the elaborate fittings which set off the colour so successfully.

Despite the advent of the entry phone and punch-card security number, the door knocker lives on as a powerful symbol, reflecting the status of the inhabitants.

Opposite:
Above left: No one would knock lightly on the fierce grotesque, grasping two dolphins firmly in his teeth and glaring out under a beetling brow on this Aix-en-Provence house.

Above right: An intricate Paris knocker is a lovely piece of conceited whimsy and fine craftsmanship.

Below left: With the arrival of regular post, letterboxes were added: this one in Florac has been pushed through the door, creating a balanced asymmetry with the knocker.

Below right: A perfect balance is achieved between this ogee-shaped decorative door panel and the simple brass knocker set geometrically above it.

This page:
Above: In rural France you might come across examples of ancient bolts like this: a wrought-iron fleur-de-lys latch fastening the door of a barn in Romme, Haute Savoie.

Below: A wooden lock and bolt holding the door of a barn in the Vallée d'Abondance in Haute Savoie. An example of the ingenuity and unconscious design ability found in French rural buildings.

To live in France without a balcony is a misfortune. Happily, many houses and most apartments have at least one. In England we hardly deserve balconies, using them for the most part for storing junk. The French, on the other hand, make full use of theirs for eating in the fresh air, sunbathing, hanging out the washing, calling out to friends, conducting romances and simply watching the world go by. Whether simple or elaborate, balconies serve an important architectural as well as social function. They break up what are often blank walls, create colour and incident, and animate dull façades.

For the French the balcony is an outdoor living room, not to mention an observation deck. One block of flats was noted to boast a wing mirror attached at an angle from one of the railings so that those apparently lounging nonchalantly on the balcony could keep a sharp eye on what was going on not only in the street below, but also on adjoining apartment balconies!

This delicate wrought-iron balcony (*opposite*) is held up by a matching herm and caryatid. Can the prim ladies sitting in its corpulent baroque setting really approve of so much naked flesh? This voluptuous house is in Aix-en-Provence.

On the right are two more balcony scenes from Provence. The balconies on one building (*top*) vary enormously both in style and in the different ways in which they are fixed to the walls. A *femme de ménage* in Menton seems set on colour coding her washing (*centre*) to the painted texture of the wall. The rough-and-ready rendering is in delicious contrast to the extreme delicacy of the balcony – sophistication and crudeness married together as so often is the case in France.

An elaborate Art Nouveau balcony (*below*) in Toulouse dates from 1900.

In England, external shutters are used only as decorative devices for houses in the outer suburbs. They have no particular function in northern climes, except perhaps for keeping out burglars, which may account for the fact that in France, whether you're in Calais or Marseilles, it's hard to find a house without them.

In southern France their widespread use is wholly explicable. Closed, louvred shutters keep the fierce afternoon sun at bay, while encouraging the circulation of fresh air and catching whatever breeze might blow. During the summer, on the hottest nights, every home seems to have them firmly locked, perhaps both as a security measure as well as to keep out the morning sun.

Architecturally, shutters perform the invaluable function of decoration, interrupting the dull uniformity of many a city block. In the crevice-like streets of the old quarters of big towns they create a lively sequence of spaces when held ajar.

Above left: In Alsace shutters play second fiddle to the lavish floral displays in window-boxes. Villages noted for their flowers are marked 'village fleuri' on signposts as you cycle or drive into them.

Centre left: A nineteenth-century brick house in Pompertuzat in Haute Garonne has open shutters, conspiring with the windows to form an unexpected arcade.

Below left: In lonely rural parts the louvred shutter gives way to the solid variety as on this house in Fontvieille, Provence. When thrown open, the shutters – with their iron bolts, catches and stays – set off the simple walls and windows of small rendered cottages.

Right: Without their shutters these eighteenth- and early-nineteenth-century seamen's houses in Le Panier, the old quarter of Marseilles, would have considerably less character. Until recently a ghetto for North African sailors and squatters, this street, like others around it, is slowly becoming gentrified.

After the commonsense plainness of English windows designed to conform to the strict lines of its architecture and to let in as much light as possible, the profusion of window styles in France is bewildering. Often they are set in plain façades. Like doors, balconies and shutters, they act as a source of decoration for many buildings. In most towns, windows tend to follow standard prototypes, but there is still a great profusion of idiosyncratic styles.

The French are particularly keen on decorating windows and house fronts with flowers – either on climbing plants or in window boxes and pots. They also have a passion for lace curtains, not the lifeless nylon variety that bedeck too many British windows, but intricate cotton ones in traditional designs which give the houses a venerable appearance. Shops of the sort you can just remember from your English childhood, where these old-fashioned fabrics can be found, are commonplace in France.

Above left: A remarkable Art Nouveau window set into a house in Alsace with a border of blue-glazed tiles enveloping a fretwork of elaborate mullions and transoms.

Centre left: Two windows have been diminished to mere gaps within an outrageous invasion of bougainvillaea, at Bormes les Mimosas in Var.

Below left: A richly decorative cotton lace runner stretched across a wooden batten.

Opposite: A grand and exotic window, almost Eastern in character, offers something more elaborate than anyone is prepared to pay for today. It's in rue Jean de Bernady, Marseilles.

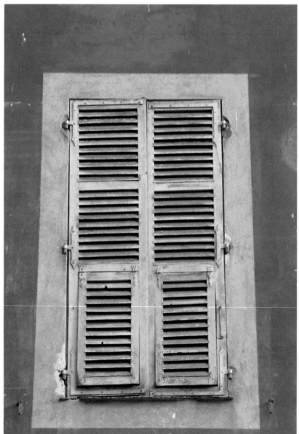

The dullest Mediterranean house can appear painterly after years of basking under a blistering sun. Pigmented *crépi* rendering applied every few years gradually fades and peels, leaving a quality of romantic decay. When the sun shines it hardly matters how faded the walls are for these houses have a memorable impact that would be lost if they were kept as primly and properly as a modern suburban house. Simply in terms of colour they are a visual treat. In England and America we would complain about houses left in this sort of condition. In France we can't see enough of them.

Areas of worn colour on this otherwise almost starkly featureless house at Macinaggio, in Corsica (*opposite above left*), turns a building's façade into a subtle complex of colour and texture. Equally charming is a sundial slowly fading into the wall of this old house in Fontvieille (*opposite above right*). It is still possible to distinguish the time as 10.30 am.

The pigments that give colour to *crépi* are natural. Not surprisingly, they harmonize well with other natural colours. The yellow maize and the blue window frame seen together in this old farmhouse wall in Ruffieux, Savoie (*opposite below left*) could hardly be better art directed.

A similarly graphic abstraction is achieved by the juxtaposition of deep ochre *crépi* on the walls, yellow paint outlining the windows and peeling blue shutters on an apartment in the old quarter of Nice (*opposite below right*).

Don't be fooled though by a rough-and-ready appearance (*above right*). If you own a house like this in Cannes you can't be that short of cash. Gentle decay adds quality and a faded façade in France often camouflages a prime property.

Deep rust-red *crépi*, recently applied, lends a splash of intense colour to the streets of Sospel, above Menton (*below right*).

201

A groaning table, lazy dogs – left waiting for a household to step out of their home near La Garde–Freinet high in the hills behind St Tropez (*above left*). Typically, the table has been placed under a shady tree, light dappling across the waiting meal. The French are expert outdoor eaters and enjoy it the more if the setting, furniture and even the crockery are as rustic as possible. Here, one gets a sense of sophistication from the cut flowers on the table.

Another dining table is set underneath a restored farmyard shed (*below left*), to ensure both food and diners do not deteriorate in the sun. The curved pink tiles of this Vaucluse house are typical of Provence.

An austere terrace in the Camargue (*right*) provides the perfect setting for lazing away a hot afternoon. This strong sheltered gallery spans the breadth of a southern farmhouse and acts as an outside living and dining room. Even with the sun at its fiercest the wonderful colonial cane chairs are kept in the shade.

It takes particularly bad weather to get the French to eat indoors if there's a chance to do so outside. They like to sit on the pavement outside city cafés, and to picnic on roadside verges, no matter how close or dense the passing traffic.

The owners of this elegant house outside St Rémy eat out every day, unless it's cold, wet and stormy, from May to October. Like most Provençals they don't care to sit directly in the sun, and choose to eat under tall, shady trees, which makes sense given their choice of antique iron furniture, which could feel like scorching gridirons if left under the direct glare of the sun.

The house dates from the sixteenth century with nineteenth-century additions. Enclosed by walls, this sheltered space is a serene open-air room. With large trees protecting the diners and food from direct wilting sunlight and wind, it is a perfect setting for enjoying a long lunch.

Unlike their often mean, cramped and carpeted counterparts in England, French halls are usually left just as their architects intended them – glorious in their stone, marble and polished wood. Often one enters a grand hallway or ascends some superb staircase only to be shown into an ill-proportioned apartment with poor taste in interior decor. The hall can be as deceiving as the exterior.

Above left: A simple tiled and whitewashed hall and stair in Salernes, Provence, constructed recently using only old materials gleaned from demolition sites.

Below left: A rickety but elegant seventeenth-century stair in rue Beauregard, Paris, at the top of which the notorious poisoner, La Voisin, premeditated ghastly murders over three hundred years ago.

Above right: A sweeping stair in the Hôtel Mansart was built by Louis XIV's architect Hardouin-Mansart in 1680 near Place des Vosges in Paris. It was recently restored by the decorator Jacques Garcia who has shown great respect for its powerful simplicity.

Below right: A wholly unspoilt early-nineteenth-century staircase in a provincial house appears more like an object of furniture than a main route through the house.

Opposite: If you're lucky enough to have an apartment in Place des Vosges, this is what your communal stair might look like. Although seemingly simple it's an immensely sophisticated essay in architectural design, creating an uninterrupted rhythm of stone, marble and wrought iron.

This page:
Above left: A simple red-tiled and ochre-washed staircase juts up through an old country house near Aix-en-Provence.

Above right: The winding medieval stair shown here is a nice deceit. It does not belong here, in this neo-Gothic house in Bougival, outside Paris, commissioned from a pupil of Viollet-le-Duc a hundred years ago. The owner wanted it to look as if the house had stood for centuries so the old stairway was installed. The treads have indeed been worn down by generations of users.

Below left: A simple, sculptural oak stair is cantilevered from the rendered walls of this converted old mill, a case of aesthetics dominating practicality.

Below right: In palatial French buildings the staircase can be totally overwhelming; this one is in a grand house in the sixteenth arrondissement. The shallow risers, though space consuming, make for an easy climb.

209

Despite their fine taste in food and wine, their love of beautiful paintings and artefacts and their historic dominance of interior style and manners in Europe, and later America, the French have placed interior decoration rather low on their list of priorities. They spend less money on furniture and household objects than most other affluent nations. Possibly this is because they have so many excellent options for entertaining and eating away from home and also because in large areas of the country they spend time outdoors. While the Italians have made enormous inroads into international furniture design and interior style in recent years, the French have lagged behind, despite government recognition of their talented interior designers demonstrated by regular refurbishment of the Elysée Palace, the official residence of the President. In England where our home is our castle, it is unlikely 10 Downing Street will become a show house for contemporary designers: we have too much respect for tradition.

Yet, as with most things, those French who have embraced modern interior design have done so with great enthusiasm. Perhaps the most important aspect of French interior design is its range and originality.

Opposite: The ultra-cool apartment of origami exponent Christian Astuguevielle shows his love of the Japanese tradition. The artist has stripped and painted these rooms so that they look as if they're fashioned from wood and paper.

This page:
Above right: A detail from the Château Halard, in the Auvergne, with bright yellow doors and traditional wallpaper, has a colourful charm.

Centre right: This guest room in a house in Charentes is simple, spare, whitewashed and tiled.

Below right: A modest country living room has simple furniture which gains character from the white sheeting and elaborate textile throws.

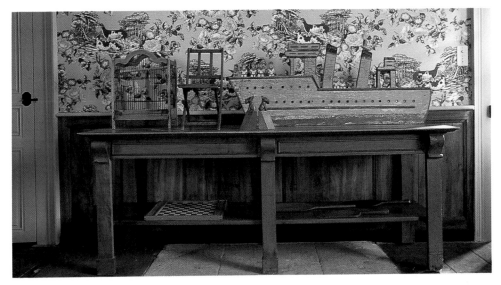

An apartment in St Tropez (*left*) shows an important aspect of French interior style – the ability to maintain the architectural proportions and detailing of a room while incorporating into it an eclectic range of objects from different periods including the very modern. This room has original oak floors providing a strong textured base; classical intricacy comes from the ceiling mouldings, the fireplace and a decorative mirror frame. The lamps and sofa have clean modern lines and in addition there are simple ceramics. They combine to create an extremely personal, warm and inviting interior. Another typical expression of French style is the use of spare rustic furniture in an utterly simple room brought to life with a colourful fan of cushions in traditional fabrics. It works particularly well in a country building such as this old farmhouse (*above*). The floor is plain polished pine providing a beautiful mellow surface unhindered by decoration on the walls or windows.

Claude Monet's wonderful house in Giverny in the Seine valley has a timeless quality. The confidence with which he used colour is legendary. The cool, strong blue of the kitchen (traditionally used throughout Brittany and Normandy) frames the bright, glowing yellow dining room (*above left*). An artist who spent most of his life experimenting with colour and light, he was able to ignore the cluttered formality of the typical nineteenth-century approach. He left broad areas of clear surface on the floors and walls – avoiding carpets and fabrics which absorb colour and add confusion. He was drawn to the rustic as the basis of his approach and the room is utterly functional and relaxed in atmosphere, without pretension or grandeur.

The same rural understatement is seen in a house in Provence (*below left*). The dining room is a straightforward, well-proportioned room decorated with Emile Garcin's magnificent collection of plates. They form a superb backdrop to the room, displayed on symmetrical wooden shelves which strongly contain the mass of colour and pattern with their defined vertical sections. The collection includes deep-green Lunéville plates, asparagus Barbotines and antique patterned brown Faucon plates from the old kilns at Apt. Monet's influence can be felt in the choice of paint and the table covering, and can be seen again in this very French salon of the same house (*right*) where a focus is created by the antique quilt covering a table. The strong simplicity is relieved by the early-nineteenth-century *faux-bambou* armchairs and the decorative mosaic floor.

Given the French preoccupation with food, the kitchen ought to be the most important room in the French home. It's the place where everyone gathers, even if the kitchen is a small Parisian galley squeezed into a modern apartment block. It seems ironical that so many modern architects this century have tried to destroy the idea of the kitchen as a family room. It's not a machine for cooking in, but one of the most attractive places to talk and eat, particularly on winter evenings.

The owners of Château Margaux in Bordeaux thought so highly of this redundant medieval kitchen (*above*) that they now use it as an informal dining room. The scrubbed stone walls, ovens and sink are warmed by the glittering display of old copper pans and cooking utensils.

Provincial crockery is designed for heavy, day-to-day use, and often carries simple, blue and white designs (*left*). It should be left on view on open shelving rather than hidden behind cupboard doors.

Durable materials give old kitchens and cooking utensils their functional appeal. One can really enjoy making a meal in a room where every surface can be scrubbed back to perfection (*above*). This is a classic kitchen of classic objects and surfaces including the solid cast-iron range, ceramic tiles, wooden plate rack, the enamelled tin coffee pot and mugs, the glistening, but obviously well used steamer, the wire vegetable basket, and the marble-topped table and bentwood chairs.

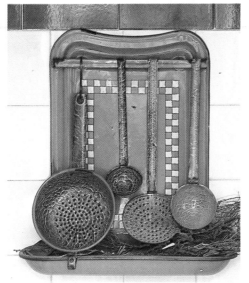

A French household enamelled tin utensil rack (*left*), complete with broad lip to collect drips, appears like a holy shrine to traditional kitchen utensils and details the lasting attraction of functional design.

French manufacturers still produce traditional designs in the original materials. Kitchens throughout the world are equipped with these French utensils that date back through centuries but remain the most practical, durable and attractive to use.

A traditional French bed (*above left*) has a comfortable voluptuousness with its square pillows, brass bedstead, and simple cotton quilt.

A grand late-eighteenth-century bed, upholstered in simple stripes, belongs to a house in Fontarèche, not far from Nîmes (*above right*), one of the best preserved ancient Roman towns in France, which might explain this owner's love of neo-classical design. But although the ideas are pretentious, drawn as they are from the French Empire style, the execution is delightfully provincial. The striped fabrics and plain materials used in the construction of the bed and the unassuming red tiled floor it stands on give the room a simple elegance.

This bedroom in a venerable château (*opposite above*) is a lovely exercise in symmetry; yet because this is a provincial scene the symmetry is not absolute. The vernacular beds sport slightly different details – the legs, for example – while the locally woven fabrics don't quite match. Any other decoration beyond flowers would spoil this beautifully balanced room.

A collection of rustic pots and urns (the Barbotine is by Cheret and dated 1870) on a bamboo table (*opposite below*) stand out like great antiques in this simple white interior. Again it expresses the French ability to mix objects with extraordinary panache, but always against a classic background – here with plain painted panelling and a fine wood floor. The room provides a lesson for anyone who is tempted to over-decorate a bedroom.

Early impressions of French bathrooms on the English visitor are likely to make one fear the worst. Aside from lavatory basins that seem to be designed the wrong way round and bidets which leave ignorant *Anglais* lost as to their purpose, the plumbing often seems more than a little antique. But just as the French seem to prefer old-fashioned, classic kitchens, so they've begun to make a virtue out of voluptuous antique bathroom fittings placed in stark modern spaces.

A spacious setting gives importance to an old enamel bath on grand cast-iron ball and claw feet (*above left*). The room is functional but quietly decorative – a perfect atmosphere in which to soak.

A bath of good proportion is matched with *lui et elle* basins (*below left*). These are big, wide and shallow, far more practical than the mean, deep little tubs that characterize modern designs. Old French basins were designed, apart from anything else, to bath baby, which is usually an ordeal for the parent and tot in a modern basin.

The spacious bathroom is taken to a wonderful conclusion with this spectacular view (*opposite*) in a Provençal villa. A stone bath and basin are offset by natural wood chair and screen echoing an early-twentieth-century delight in geometric decorative detailing. There is a glamorous appeal in a beautiful bathroom that has been given priority in a house. It should be the most relaxing and indulgent of places. The quality of bathroom materials and the simple functionalism for which it should be designed, offer a chance for style at its best.

NORMANDIE
LE HAVRE – SOUTHAMPTON – NEW YORK

L'affiche la plus célèbre : celle
de Cassandre, dessinée en 193

gée, sublimé par l
de l'époque. Il n
bjets, quelques m
ostalgie d'un certai

FRENCH BY DESIGN

French design hovers curiously between the primitive and the sophisticated, the agricultural and the urban, the intellectual and the artistic. This reflects something of the great divide in France between town and country, or perhaps more accurately, between Paris and the rest. France is still a remarkably agricultural country. The idea of the suburb, and its effect on society as a whole and design in particular, is quite a recent phenomenon and still largely confined to a ring around Paris. Even then it is a kind of suburbia taken to wild extremes and nothing like the garden suburbs surrounding London or Birmingham, or the sprawling conurbations stretching out from New York or Los Angeles.

Interestingly, some of the very best French design is a resolution of these contradictions. You have only to look at the curious Citroën 2CV – perhaps the most distinctive French design this century. The design team was masterminded by Pierre Boulanger and headed by André Lefebvre, with the distinctive body shape created by Flaminio Bertoni. They managed to combine rustic simplicity with urban sophistication. The car is as much a farm hut as it is an umbrella on wheels. In appearance it seems very primitive, and was actually designed to carry sacks of potatoes and pigs across bumpy fields and along unmetalled roads. Yet the thinking behind it and some of the engineering – in particular the engine and suspension – were notably innovative. When it appeared in 1948, after its production had been interrupted by the war, it was also the first car in Europe to be produced as the result of major market research. It proved that marketing is a vital ingredient in the selling of goods, however complex or simple. The first prototype appeared fifty years ago and only now is its continued production threatened. For decades it has been selling as a smart, compact and practical town car, as a chic fashion accessory as much as a work-horse. Underneath its basic rural shell lurks an urbane car.

French design after the Second World War seemed to slip away from the kind of happy compromise that makes the 2CV so satisfying. Awakening from the stultifying war years, and faced with an influx of American soldiers, Marshall Plan aid and foreign ideas, they embraced the modern way of life almost obsessively, as if trying to prove that France could be more modern than any nation. Some of the new architecture seemed designed to find favour with film directors looking for backdrops for avant-garde films, but hardly with society at large. New housing schemes are still taken to absurd conclusions. When the French embrace post-modern or neo-classical styles they try to outdo the Americans and the Italians.

The French worship the artist and the intellectual. There is a deep-rooted love of rational thinking in France, but it engenders the sort of rationalism that leads to revolution – whether in art, design or politics. This shows in the work of fashion designers and of great artist/intellectuals like Le Corbusier. Corbusier started his career designing crisp, white, rational 'machines for living', but in later years his buildings were a mixture of the raw, the rich and the poetic.

Philippe Starck is the only contemporary French furniture designer to achieve international repute. Yet even he adopts the role of artist. He does not seem much interested in structure and function, and in fact his work is often wilful and abstract. Viewed as art objects, however, his pieces are lovely things.

It is rather a relief to get away from overheated urban design, and return to the simplicity of the French countryside. Basic, everyday design in modern France still holds a great appeal. After Paris, with its haute couture, grandiose architecture and clever art, the old-fashioned virtues of rural France come into their own.

There is a side to the French character that is deeply conservative, and this has ensured that the best traditional objects are still manufactured and in daily use. One could not improve on the design of a cast-iron casserole or an ancient shop façade, both of which sit happily in modern France alongside the very new, the chic and the innovative. This deep respect for tradition is also a respect for simple, functional and effective design, and it is reflected in many of the best basic objects – such as the BIC pen and the Cricket lighter.

It is when French design successfully combines conservatism and revolution, urbanity and rusticity, that it is at its best and commands world respect.

In his 1958 film, *Mon Oncle* (*left, above and below*), Jacques Tati teased and mocked the contemporary French obsession with all things modern, American, plastic, convenient and technocratic. Tati's film was an hilarious and necessary commentary on the worship of the 'new', which throughout the the 1950s and 1960s had to be adopted at all costs. You could say that French culture was in danger of being raped then. It seems remarkable that so much that is good has survived. Once the French decide to do something, they do not hesitate and test the water first, but jump in with total conviction. It is no bad thing as a rule, since it provides an outlet and expression for new ideas. When Louis XIV, Napoleon, Giscard d'Estaing, Pompidou or Mitterand commissioned a project, it had to be the most daring in Europe, like Versailles or the Arc de Triomphe, the conversion of the Gare d'Orsay, the Centre Pompidou or the pyramid at the Louvre.

What *Mon Oncle* highlights is that when this dedication to things new goes seriously wrong, it is because the French look abroad for inspiration. Things American were created for a new and suburban society – in France the same ideas appear absurd. The *style Américain* was superimposed onto a country with its own long traditions in design. Until the last war, France had been leading the way with new innovations and designs, but after it there was panic because that lead had been lost. Instead of waiting for their own designers to catch up, the French adopted alien ideas. This resulted in extremism for its own sake.

La Grande Borne (*top right*), on the outskirts of Paris, has a real fascination, and is one of the most extreme but interesting achievements in postwar architecture.

The Centre Pompidou appears to be an expression of the same extremism, but it is, in fact, part of the long tradition of innovation. It took courage for the French President to act on his word and actually commission the avant-garde architectural team of Richard Rogers and Renzo Piano to build this vast red and blue high-tech building right in the heart of Paris. It is a remarkable and admirable building, yet it sadly contravenes the far-sighted sanity which had previously prevailed: that modern buildings be placed outside central Paris. It replaced a charming collection of old brothels and cheap hotels, no longer needed once the markets had departed from Les Halles to Rungis.

It was a serious mistake to destroy the old market buildings which, whilst they could no longer function in modern Paris, could have been effectively converted. Instead, a preposterous complex of subterranean shops was installed which make the point loud and clear that they are modern and progressive (*centre right*). There is a danger of being seduced by this type of insensitive modernity, also seen at La Défense and in the vast *hypermarchés* on the outskirts of every major town. Equally insidious is the plain kitsch of some modern buildings such as those in *Mon Oncle* or this ridiculous seafront housing (*below right*) at La Baule in Brittany.

So why did a country so adept at the art of embracing the new allow their enthusiasm to get out of hand? It is a contradiction typical of France. It happened at a time when many European countries allowed similar atrocities to take place. Part of the problem was the desire to keep in step with the rest of the world and, undoubtedly, it was partially economic. During a recession it was convenient to use cheap materials and slick designs to give a gloss of modernity that soon deteriorated into ugliness. At least the French had the capacity to laugh at themselves as they did it.

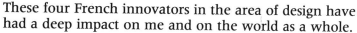

These four French innovators in the area of design have had a deep impact on me and on the world as a whole.

Andrée Putman is the embodiment of good taste which she wears like a mantle. I remember admiring a house she had designed for herself back in the late 1950s when she was working in magazines. Her talent lies in her infallible eye which detects quality and elegance at a glance. In her work as an interior designer she has the ability, as no one else, to combine luxury and practicality. Having created the settings she wants, she then manufactures the furniture and objects to place in them.

With her company, Ecart International, she has brought back the work of Eileen Gray, Fortuny, Jean-Michel Franck and Gaudí, recreating sofas, door handles, chairs, tables and lamps which, timeless in their design, fit well into today's interiors. Having tracked down and selected the best in design, she has the astute, timely, marketing skills and the influence to bring them to a wide market.

Denise Fayolle was the first person to appreciate the implications and importance of design in mass distribution. In the early 1950s, she joined Prisunic. With over eleven million customers and numerous branches, the store, through her efforts, was completely restyled and in doing so she revolutionized mass retailing in France.

At the time, mass market and good taste were regarded as mutually incompatible. Denise struggled with the manufacturers and her own colleagues to improve design and, at the head of a great team, she organized the redesign of the stores and the repackaging of 22,000 items, produced a catalogue of furnishings and created *Style Prisu*, a vehicle for immediate success, marrying marketing and design to enormous effect. I first met her in the early 1960s when she asked me to design furniture Prisunic as part of the range.

In 1967 she established the Mafia agency with Maïmé Arnodin, and has spent the last twenty years acting as a link between designers and traders, as well as creating an influential advertising agency.

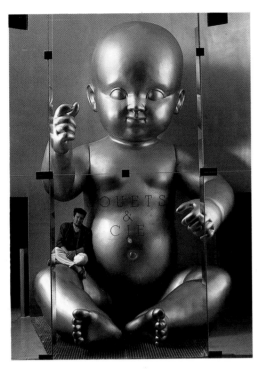

Philippe Starck will be fifty in the year 2000. After spending ten years travelling, snoozing and scribbling, he created a role for himself 'mediatizing architecture'. His inspiration comes from diverse fields – sociology, electronics, sex, politics – and as a great artist/designer he has succeeded with enormous wit, humour, energy and downright impishness. His designs have included such fashionable places in Paris as the Bains Douches, the Main Bleue and the famous Café Costes where he created every detail of the interior including the furniture and the extraordinary lavatories – the gents' urinal is a luminous fountain combining a play of glass, light and water. He has designed President Mitterrand's private apartments at the Elysée Palace and has worked with many international companies, including Japanese electronics firms. His furniture is not always exclusive – his designs appear in Habitat stores and in the *Trois Suisses* catalogue – and not always practical. His success stems from his determination to follow no lead but his own and to live unashamedly in the present, free from nostalgia.

Marie-Paule Pellé is an internationally unrivalled master for her knowledge of everything to do with interior design. Born in Orléans, she came to Paris and began her career in the early 1970s, bringing her already exceptional talent to the newly created *La Maison de Marie Claire*. Here she showed ways for readers to improve their immediate environment by freeing themselves from rigid terms of social reference, demonstrating that modern design could be affordable and desirable. She was in demand as a stylist all over Europe and went on to influence such magazines as the superb *100 Idées*.

In the early 1980s she left the popular market to set up *Décoration Internationale* – an exclusive and sophisticated interiors magazine of enormous influence. Alexander Liberman, the legendary artistic power behind Condé Nast, took her to New York where she became an ambassador for European taste, new styles in interior design, and for all new ideas coming out of the European continent. More recently she even found time to direct a new magazine in Paris, *Vogue Décoration*.

French fashion design continues to dominate the world, not least because there is a constant flow of talented designers and a tradition of craftsmanship.

Top left: Poiret was a revolutionary who abandoned corsets in favour of soft, high-waisted dresses. (1914)

Top centre: Schiaparelli popularized man-made materials, zippers and shocking pink. (1937)

Top right: Christian Dior's New Look sent out a message of femininity not feminism, clinching waists above sweeping skirts. (1947)

Centre left: It took a comeback from the legendary Coco Chanel to give the new career girl her uniform of short straight skirt, neat suit and little black dress. (1968)

Centre: Courrèges showed the mini first, in 1964. (1967)

Centre right: Yves Saint Laurent remains the most consistent and innovative modern designer. (1977)

Below left: Sonia Rykiel's unstructured knits inspired a new generation. (1985)

Below centre: Jean-Paul Gaultier – most influential designer of the 1980s. (1985)

Below right: Azzedine Alaia makes a virtue of a curvaceous figure and a sexy walk. (1986)

Opposite: Givenchy cut the city suit into a new sophistication. (1950s)

229

Step into a new Paris clothes shop and you'll find yourself an actor on a very bare stage. The shops are big, dramatic warehouses where assistants, often very beautiful, are there to show off the latest styles and not to bother customers with hard sell.

Above left: Yohji Yamamoto's shop in rue du Louvre, designed to look unfinished. Concrete floors are lit dramatically by tough industrial spotlights, creating a factory-like aesthetic aimed at showing off the clothes, not the interior.

Below left: Western House, owned by Marithé and François Girbaud, in rue Etienne Marcel, is less extreme. Designed by decorators Michel Hamon and Antonia Astori, it is a warmer industrial style. Smooth, polished floors replace Yamamoto's concrete. There are even chairs to sit on (designed by Mallet-Stevens), while subtle downlights punctuate the white ceiling.

Right: The Jean-Paul Gaultier shop in Galerie Vivienne reveals a mix of styles contrasting a harsh, industrial, modern Japanese imagery with quotes from classical antiquity. Robot mannequins, born of steel and epoxy resin, twist and grimace from their bases set into repro fragments of mosaic floors from Pompeii.

We go to France for the shops as much as anything else. The old shops struggle on despite new developments. In England we have virtually nothing like them, except in exclusive areas of London. In this respect, the French, like the Italians, seem to have got their priorities right. Keep the workaday superstores on the edge of town where you can load up the car with basic household goods and leave the centre of town for the specialist and convenience shop, where sensual and immediate gratification is all.

All the shops shown here have one thing in common: we can't wait to go inside. Often set into old façades, the shop fronts stand out with their handsome nameboards, graphics, paintwork and displays. There's a touching appeal in even the shabbiest traditional shop.

In England, the general run of provincial shops is banal and tacky, and many long-established retailers have destroyed irreplaceable original shop fronts.

Maybe it is because of a deep-rooted respect for tradition that, having satisfied the upwardly mobile and avaricious with huge and vulgar *hypermarchés*, France still provides shops where the customer emerges with a neatly wrapped and tied parcel, feeling special and pampered.

Opposite:
Above left: A grocery shop in the centre of a Normandy village.

Above right: A traditional boulangerie, in rue Losserand in Paris.

Centre left: An angler's shop in Limon, in the Aude region.

Centre right: Crisp cotton blinds announce a grocery shop.

Below left: Vignal has sold soap and oil in Marseilles since 1905.

Below right: A hardware shop in Avignon built in the 1960s.

Right: Eighteenth-century designs for a shop and a restaurant façade.

Boutique de M. Bertin M^{de} de Modes rue de la Loi N°26

Boutique de M^r. Emerie Limonadier Boulevard du Temple.

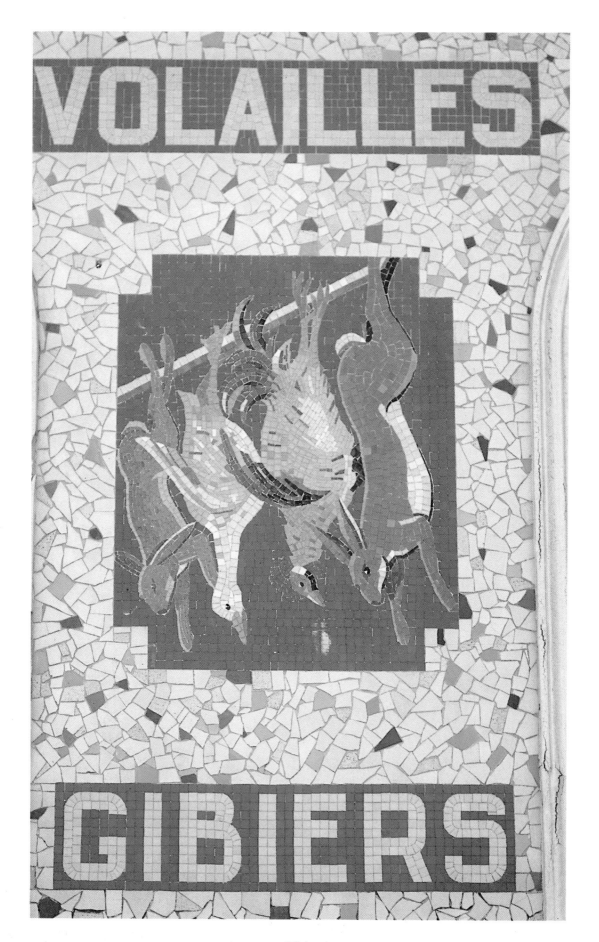

In London only the Michelin building — French, of course, but with some recent British refinements — echoes the richness of French shop decoration, widespread at the turn of the century. This type of decoration enjoyed its heyday between the mid-1850s and the First World War, after which the restraints of Modernism replaced decorative detailing with graphic purity.

The poultry and game mosaic, in Nice, is very much to the point, but the glass paintings in Paris, still there to be seen, present romantic views of the goods within. Slaughtering cattle seems quite palatable when we're presented with a pastoral scene of a contented cow.

In a tough industrial world these images were designed as small escapes from city pressures; as sweet deceits. None of them is great art, but a popular tradition aimed to brighten the city and bring the source of the produce, the countryside, closer to the urban shopper.

Opposite: A mosaic design from the 1930s on a poulterer's shop in Nice.

This page:
Above left: A bakery in Faubourg St Martin, Paris.

Above right: A rural scene on a shop in rue Ordener, Paris.

Below left: A painting on glass decorates a butcher's in rue de Passy, Paris.

Below right: A detail from a bread shop in rue Ledru Rollin, Paris.

A shop sign is worth a thousand words. There is no mistaking what the various shops are selling, except perhaps for the rabbit holding up what only reveals itself to be a light bulb announcing an electrical store.

The tradition dates from Roman times when hops would be hung outside taverns to say that new beer was on tap, and that idea developed in the Middle Ages. In France, unlike Britain, the tradition has never died. The effects range from the macabre to the downright whimsical.

Above left: A locksmith's near Chinon.

Above right: Monsieur Bibendum announcing Michelin tyres.

Centre left: An electrical shop in Alsace.

Centre right: A neon pig above a charcuterie in Les Halles.

Below left: An old hat shop in Rodez, Aveyron.

Below right: A horse butcher's in Paris.

Opposite: The Escargot restaurant in Paris.

In France, despite a continuing programme of rationalization, road signs are far more idiosyncratic and *ad hoc* than in Britain. They add considerably to the charm of small towns, and it can be argued that they don't need replacing as long as they are perfectly serviceable. Even standard signs seen at the entrance, and exit, of every town and village, have a distinctive typography. In Paris, the blue and white, enamelled, street name-plates have become a symbol of the city and it would be folly to change them.

Above left: The classic enamelled sign denoting a Paris street name.

Centre left: The clear typography and route numbering which typifies French road signs, here in Bonnieux, Vaucluse.

Below left: An old milestone stands on a pass in the Pyrenees.

Right: A wonderful faded painted wall advertising Lu biscuits dominates the sign announcing the boundary of Le Havre.

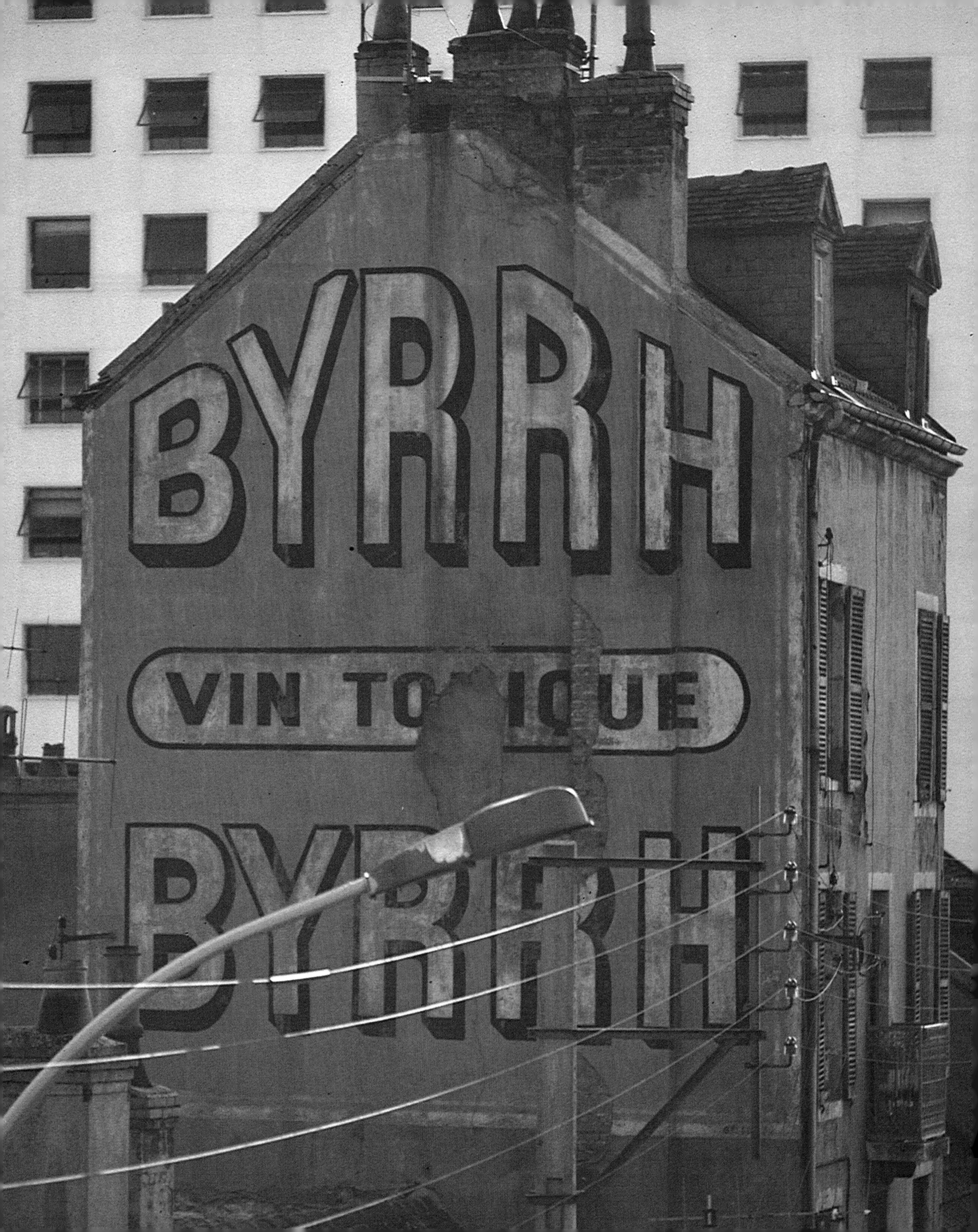
BYRRH
VIN TO IQUE
BYRRH

Street advertising is far less controlled in France and Italy than it is in England.

Advertisers painted walls before the advent of the printed bill-board, and many have survived as painted memories of advertising styles of the past. Byrrh's Vin Tonique will be publicized on this old apartment block in Dijon (*opposite*) until a property speculator destroys the building.

In Pont Audemer, in Normandy, an advertising panel was put up at the beginning of this century (*above left*) with a border of ceramic tiles – a delightful design which has withstood the rigours of time.

The Dubonnet advert (*above right*) dates from 1932 and is the work of the brilliant poster designer, Cassandre. Normally elevated to museums of graphic art, here it is in Paris fifty-five years on, still plugging the ruby-red drink.

Enamelled tin advertisements have also enjoyed a long life, but they continue to have relevance since the logos they display are as enduring as the advertising signs. They add character to this village street in Périgord (*centre*).

An ad hoc mixture of advertising is seen in most French town centres today, as here (*below left*) in Paris where the poster man is busy with his paste. Bill stickers obviously meet intense competition as they create a fascinating and ever-changing urban wallpaper (*below right*).

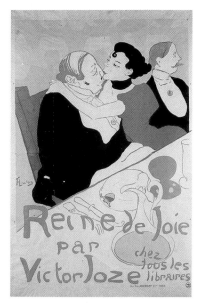

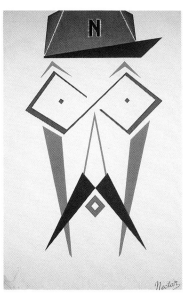

French poster art is exactly that – a fine art – which reached its peak in the 1930s when Kiffer, Cassandre and Fix-Masseau dominated the field.

Opposite:

Top left: Amorous late-nineteenth-century poster by Toulouse-Lautrec advertising Victor Joze's book 'Reine de Joie', 1892.

Top centre: The first appearance of the Michelin man, Monsieur Bibendum, in Marius Galop's poster of 1911.

Top right: Wagon-lit poster by Cassandre, 1929.

Centre left: Poster by Gaston Girbal for an Edith Piaf concert, Paris, 1935.

Centre: Maurice Chevalier poster by Charles Kiffer, 1936.

Centre right: Bally shoes, 1934, by Leonette Cappiello.

Below left: Banania drinking chocolate. Anonymous, 1959.

Below centre: Early use of photo-montage for Pernod, by Cassandre, 1934.

Below right: Poster of 'Nectar', for Nicolas wines by Claude Lemeunier, 1938.

Right: Poster advertising the Spanish dancer, Herrera, by Joël Martel, 1926.

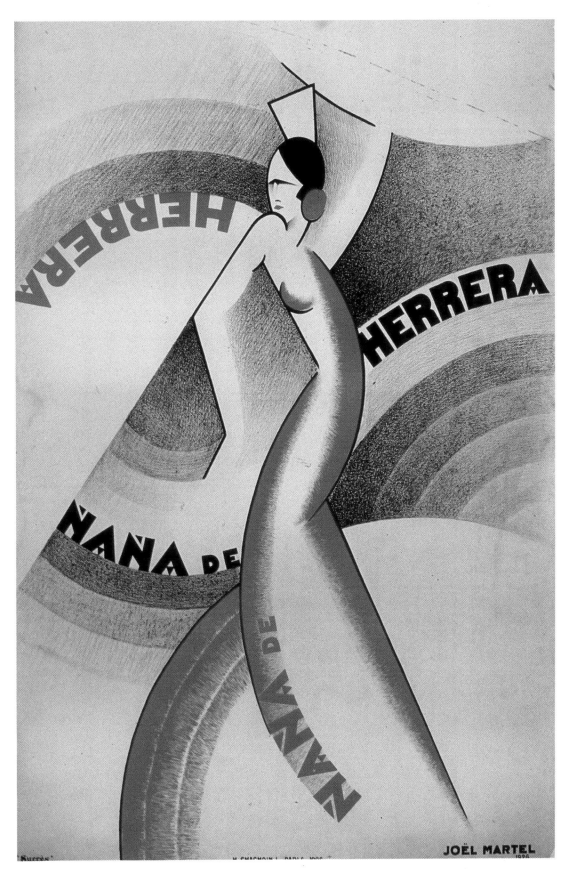

Contemporary advertising continues the high standards set in France since the late nineteenth century and has a distinctively French imagery. Photography now plays a major role, reflecting the best of modern magazines, but the illustrator is still of enormous importance, often clearly influenced by the great poster artists of the 1920s and 1930s.

Opposite:
Above left: Poster for the elegant store, Au Printemps, 1984.

Above right: Perrier poster by Bernard Villemot, 1982.

Below left: Press advertising for DIM stockings, 1986.

Below right: An illustration advertising Lu biscuits by the legendary Folon, 1986.

This page:
Above: Poster designed for RATP for an exhibition, 'Le musée a le ticket' at the Musée de la Publicité in Paris, March 1983.

Below: Poster by Références for Chantal Thomass, 1987.

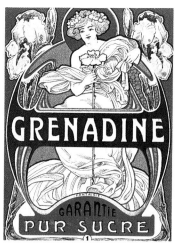

Decorative packaging has a long life in France. The French know a good thing when they see it and food packaging once established hardly changes.

Above: An alluring, Hollywood-style French maid tempting you to eat Normandy Camembert.

Top left: Olive oil label dating from 1910.

Top right: A grenadine label from 1900.

Right: The Lu Petit-Beurre biscuits poster shows their range of tins and packets available in 1900, when this poster was designed by Victor Bocchino.

Classic French design may summon up in one's mind a Louis XIV chair, Haussmann's plan of Paris or a sumptuous evening gown created by Christian Dior for a modern princess. Yet, for me, France reaches the height of its expertise in design in its everyday objects, utility products, and packaging for mass market merchandise. So much of what we admire, so much of its influence internationally and so much of its innovation has been assimilated into everyday things we take for granted.

The simplicity of the approach seems almost too obvious. When the French want to be taken seriously, whether in designing a book, a quality newspaper or a label for a fine bottle of wine, they leave well alone and adopt a purely classical approach. *Le Monde* is positively old-fashioned in its typography, and Gallimard would not consider tampering with its creamy book jackets and classic typography.

Good, wholesome food is placed in rustic packaging behind traditional labels which imply that the contents are unchanging and free of modern additives.

The cinema is important in French culture and this is reflected in designs dating from the 1930s and 1940s – the Gitanes packet has the allure of the *films noirs* in which heroes emerged from behind a screen of cigarette smoke. Cartoons and comics are also influential, reflected in bright images and colourful typography.

Some of the great French classics are incredibly basic, given mass appeal with a design that lets the simplicity speak for itself and the product withstand the ravages of fashion and changing taste. Who would want, or need, to improve the neat BIC ballpoint pen or the Cricket lighter. Both are plastic disposables with a timeless appeal.

The French have a way of turning something earthy into something sophisticated because it is well made, uses good materials and is utterly practical, yet has no pretension or decorative detailing that may clash with one's own style – hence the incredible success of Le Creuset pans and the Citroën 2CV.

But when a product wants to sing out that it has class and quality, a designer creates a classic form for its outward appearance. The Perrier bottle contains only water, but is presented with great panache. Another brilliant glass shape is the Chanel No. 5 bottle – there are a thousand well-packaged perfumes, but that bottle, whether in its smallest or largest form, is sheer, classic perfection.

It is a tribute to the French as a nation that they respect the virtues of their great traditions; they make ordinary, everyday objects a pleasure to possess and continue to give us classic products to treasure – or to throw away when we have finished with them.

Le Monde

BIC – the ballpoint pen created by Baron Bic and first made in 1950.

Ricard plays on tradition for its bottle of pastis, listing awards on its label. The modern appeal of the ashtray reflects its era of the 1950s; the water carafe, designed in 1965, takes the colourful typography and reinterprets the angular lines of the ashtray.

Originally called Tubagaz, the Cricket lighter, the first disposable, was created by the Dupont company, but is now owned by Feudor.

Gauloises – preferring the chic of crushable style – packet graphics by Jacno in 1946, complete with cartoon Gaul.

Bonne Maman jam, Pommery mustard – giving a message of good, wholesome, rustic quality.

Perrier – bottle designed 1906 and inspired by a wooden club used for body building by St John Harmsworth, the Englishman who owned the rights to bottle the water.

Lu biscuits

Traditional wood package and rustic label for La Cloche D'Or madeleines – the same since 1760.

Kub appeared in an all-red presentation in 1907 and the original design was adapted for the relaunch of Kub Or in 1958.

La Vache Qui Rit – cheese adopting light-hearted comic relief for the supermarket shelf.

Le Petit Marseillais – pure olive oil soap, unchanged for over a hundred years.

Camembert given the authority of Napoleon.

Traditional packaging for traditional foods.

Gitanes – packet graphics by Max Ponty, 1947.

Classic white porcelain.

The cafetière – abstract functionalism, designed by Italian Calimani, 1933, and refined over the years.

The champagne bottle robbed of its grandeur without a label – simple symmetry and a utilitarian battened cork. The bottle was originally more bulbous, but this shape was adopted in the 1880s.

Hexagonal, heavy porcelain coffee cup and saucer, used in cafés throughout France.

Porcelain salad bowl.

Carbon-steel, folding-blade knife, designed by Joseph Opinel in 1909, in Albiez le Vieux, near Lyons.

Soup bowl.

Coffee bowl.

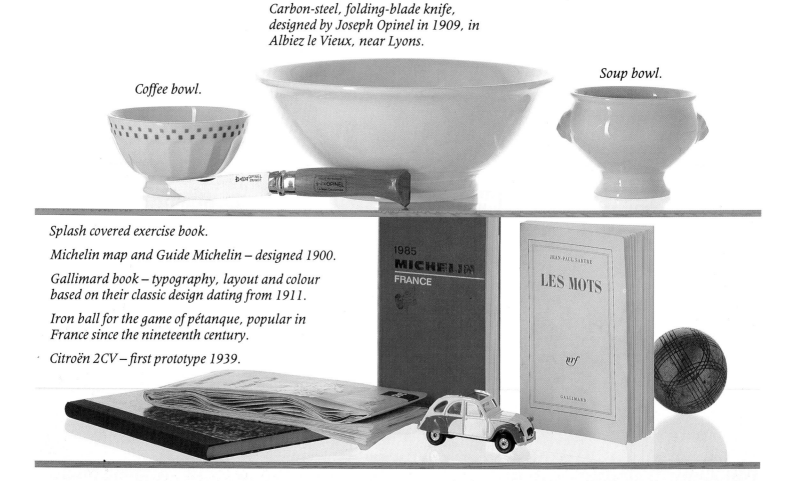

Splash covered exercise book.

Michelin map and Guide Michelin – designed 1900.

Gallimard book – typography, layout and colour based on their classic design dating from 1911.

Iron ball for the game of pétanque, popular in France since the nineteenth century.

Citroën 2CV – first prototype 1939.

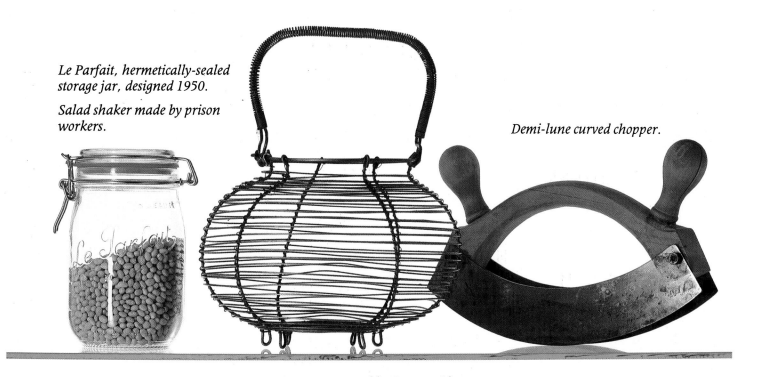

Le Parfait, hermetically-sealed storage jar, designed 1950.

Salad shaker made by prison workers.

Demi-lune curved chopper.

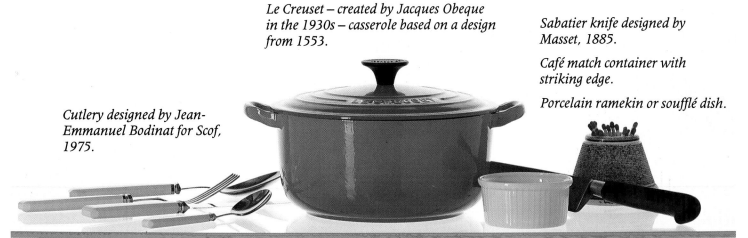

Le Creuset – created by Jacques Obeque in the 1930s – casserole based on a design from 1553.

Cutlery designed by Jean-Emmanuel Bodinat for Scof, 1975.

Sabatier knife designed by Masset, 1885.

Café match container with striking edge.

Porcelain ramekin or soufflé dish.

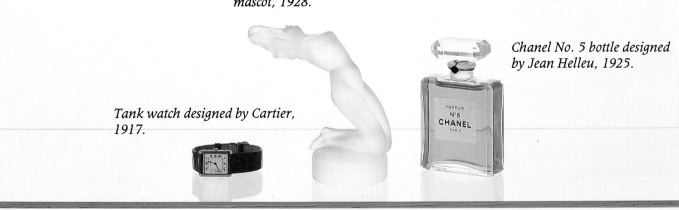

Lalique glass – designed as a car mascot, 1928.

Chanel No. 5 bottle designed by Jean Helleu, 1925.

Tank watch designed by Cartier, 1917.

INDEX

254

The publisher thanks the following photographers and organizations for their permission to reproduce the photographs in this book which are listed by page number:

1 Guy Bouchet; 2 Raymond de Seynes; 3 Christian Sarramon; 4 Gilles de Chabaneix; 6 Sir Terence Conran; 8 above Sabine Weiss/ Rapho; 8 centre Rex Features/SIPA/Nicolas; 8 below Alain Kubacsi/Explorer; 9 above left Tessa Traeger; 9 above right Denis Hughes-Gilbey; 9 centre left John Garrett; 9 centre right Denis Hughes-Gilbey; 9 below left Richard Kalvar/Magnum/John Hillelson Agency; 9 below right Chito/ANA/John Hillelson Agency; 10 above left Germain/ Rapho; 10 above centre Christian Errath/ Explorer; 10 above right Alex MacLean/ Conran Octopus; 10 centre left Jeannine Niepce/Rapho; 10 centre Alexandre Bailhache; 10 centre right Michelangelo Durazzo/ANA/John Hillelson Agency; 10 below left Hervé Gloaguen/Rapho; 10 below centre Jean-Paul Dumontier; 10 below right Hervé Gloaguen/Rapho; 11 Miss Selfridge; 12 above Dick Scott Stewart; 12 centre Patrick Ward; 12 below Guy Bouchet; 13 above Christian Sarramon; 13 centre Michael Busselle; 13 below Bruno Barbey/Magnum/John Hillelson Agency; 14 above Alex MacLean/Conran Octopus; 14 below Jacques Gayard/REA; 14–15 Daily Telegraph Colour Library/ Graham Harrison; 16 above left John Heseltine; 16 above right Denis Hughes-Gilbey; 16 centre left Christian Sarramon; 16 centre right Alexandre Bailhache/ Conran Octopus; 16 below right Michelangelo Durazzo/ANA/John Hillelson Agency; 16 below right Robert Harding Picture Library/Christine Gascoigne; 17 Jean-Paul Dumontier; 18 Dick Scott Stewart; 19 above left Rex Features/SIPA/Stumpf; 19 above right Ernst Haas/Magnum/John Hillelson Agency; 19 centre left Jean-Paul Dumontier; 19 centre right Alex MacLean/ Conran Octopus; 19 below left Dick Scott Stewart; 19 below right Alex MacLean/ Conran Octopus; 20 above Guy Bouchet; 20 below Susan Griggs Agency/Adam Woolfitt; 21 above Caroline Lespinasse/REA; 21 below Jean-Noël Reichel/Agence Top; 22 Sir Terence Conran; 24 Zefa Picture Library; 25 left Musée de la Publicité – Paris; 25 above right Jean-Paul Dumontier; 25 below right Susan Griggs Agency/Cotton Coulson; 26 Denis Hughes-Gilbey; 27 Serge Chirol; 28 left Raymond de Seynes; 28 right Philippe Perdereau and Brigitte Thomas; 28–29 Robert Harding Picture Library/Walter Rawlings; 30 above Philippe Perdereau and Brigitte Thomas; 30 centre Alexandre Bailhache; 30 below The Photographers' Library; 31 Patrick Eagar; 32 above Georges Carde/Explorer; 32 centre Anne Gaël; 32 below Denis Hughes-Gilbey; 33 Gilles de Chabaneix; 34–35 Francis Jalain/Explorer; 35 Philippe Perdereau and Brigitte Thomas; 36 Philippe Perdereau; 37 Peter Baistow; 38 Michèle Lamontagne; 39 Philippe Perdereau; 40–41 Philippe Perdereau and Brigitte

Thomas; 42 above Georges Carde/Explorer; 42 below Musée de la Publicité – Paris (© DACS, 1987); 43 Guy Bouchet; 44 left Art Directors Photo Library; 44 right Homer Sykes; 45 above Bachoffner/Gamma/Frank Spooner; 45 below Homer Sykes; 46 top Philip Plisson/Explorer; 46 above Neil Holmes; 46 below Andy Hasson; 46 bottom Francis Jalain/Explorer; 46–47 Joël Ducange/Agence Top 48 above Pascal Hinous/Agence Top; 48 centre Jean-Paul Dumontier; 48 below Christian Weiss/REA; 48–49 Christian Weiss/REA; 50 above Susan Griggs Agency/John G Ross; 50 below Anthony Blake Photo Library; 51 above left Robert Estall; 51 above right Jean Gaumy/ Magnum/John Hillelson Agency; 51 below Luc Choquer/VU; 52 above Eric Rocel/REA; 52 below Pierre Hussenot/Agence Top; 53 Hervé Gloaguen/Rapho; 54–55 Guy Bouchet; 56 above left Anne Gaël; 56 above right Christian Sarramon; 56 centre left Raymond de Seynes; 56 centre right Denis Hughes-Gilbey; 56 below left Robert Tixador/Agence Top; 56 below right Henri Cartier-Bresson/Magnum/John Hillelson Agency; 57 Denis Hughes-Gilbey; 58 above Christian Sarramon; 58 below Eddy Posthuma de Boer; 59 above Susan Griggs Agency/Adam Woolfitt; 59 below Raymond de Seynes; 60–61 Sir Terence Conran; 63 Rosine Mazin/Agence Top; 64–65 Norman Parkinson Ltd; 66 Lauros – Giraudon/Art Institute of Chicago (© ADAGP, 1987); 67 left Jean-Paul Dumontier; 67 right BBC Hulton Picture Library; 68 Jean-Philippe Charbonnier/Agence Top; 69 Rosine Mazin/ Agence Top; 70–71 Yann Arthus-Bertrand/ Explorer; 72 above Raymond de Seynes; 72 below Christian Sarramon; 73 Rosine Mazin/Agence Top; 74 above Rex Features/ SIPA/Stumpf; 74 centre Christian Sarramon; 74 below Rosine Mazin/Agence Top; 75 Christian Sarramon; 76–77 Yann Arthus-Bertrand/Explorer; 78 above Patrick Lorne/Explorer; 78 below Gilles de Chabaneix; 79 Alex MacLean/Conran Octopus; 80 above left Francis Jalain/ Explorer; 80 above right Alex MacLean/ Conran Octopus; 80 centre Alex MacLean/ Conran Octopus; 80 below left Alex MacLean/Conran Octopus; 80 below right François Le Diascorn/Agence Top; 81 Raymond de Seynes; 82–83 Jean-Pierre Couderc/Agence Top; 84 Jean-Paul Nacivet/ Explorer; 85 Jean-Paul Dumontier; 86 above Gilles de Chabaneix; 86 below Andrej Reiser/Bilderberg; 87 above Rex Features/SIPA/Stumpf; 87 below Rex Features/SIPA; 88 above Rosine Mazin/ Agence Top; 88 centre Serge Korniloff; 88 below Serge Korniloff; 89 Serge Korniloff; 90 Sir Terence Conran; 92 Terry McCormick/ Conran Octopus; 92 inset Gilles de Chabaneix; 93 above Philippe Perdereau and Brigitte Thomas; 93 centre Francis Jalain/Explorer; 93 below Jean-Paul Dumontier; 94 above Philippe Perdereau and Brigitte Thomas; 94 below Robert Estall; 94–95 Christian Sarramon; 96 above Michael Busselle; 96 below Denis Hughes-

Gilbey; 97 above Alexandre Bailhache; 97 below The Image Bank/Peter Miller; 98–105 Alex MacLean/Conran Octopus; 106 Hervé Gloaguen/Rapho; 107 above Philippe Perdereau and Brigitte Thomas; 107 centre Christian Sarramon; 107 below Jean-Paul Dumontier; 108 above Remi Michel/Rapho; 108 below Jean-Paul Dumontier; 109 above Denis Hughes-Gilbey; 109 centre Joël Ducange/Agence Top; 109 below Jacques Gayard/REA; 110 above Denis Hughes-Gilbey; 110 below Retrograph Archive Collection, London; 111 above Robert Estall; 111 below Rosine Mazin/ Agence Top; 112 above Caroline Lespinasse/ REA; 112 below Christian Sarramon; 113 above Philippe Roy/Explorer; 113 below Jean-Paul Dumontier; 114 above Jean-Paul Dumontier; 114 centre Anne Gaël; 114 below Raymond de Seynes; 115 Susan Griggs Agency/Adam Woolfitt; 116 Rosine Mazin/Agence Top; 117 above Christian Sarramon; 117 centre Jacques Gayard/REA; 117 below Robert Harding Picture Library/ Michael H Black; 118 above Jacques Gayard/REA; 118 below Jean-Guy Jules/ ANA/John Hillelson Agency; 119 above Rosine Mazin/Agence Top; 119 below The Image Bank/Bernard Roussell; 120 Rosine Mazin/Agence Top; 121 above Christian Sarramon; 121 centre Jacques Gayard/REA; 121 below Christian Sarramon; 122 Michael Busselle; 122-3 Charlie Waite/Landscape Only; 124–125 Jean-Paul Dumontier; 126 above left Denis Hughes-Gilbey; 126 above right Christian Sarramon; 126 below Christian Sarramon; 127 Christian Sarramon; 128 above left Robert Harding Picture Library/Robert Cundy; 128 above right La Maison de Marie Claire/Gilles de Chabaneix; 128 centre left Lavalette/Vloo; 128 centre right Sellier/Vloo; 128 below left B Thomas/Explorer; 128 below right Philippe Perdereau; 129 Christian Sappa/ CEDRI; 130 above left Christian Sarramon; 130 above right Charlie Waite/Landscape Only; 130 centre left Francis Jalain/ Explorer; 130 below Christian Sarramon; 131 Christian Sarramon; 132 above Susan Griggs Agency/Monique Jacot; 132 below Denis Hughes-Gilbey; 133 above Guy Bouchet; 133 below Stafford Cliff; 134 Christian Sarramon; 135 left Christian Sarramon; 135 right Hervé Gloaguen/ Rapho; 136 Jean-Erik Pasquier/Rapho; 137 Serge Korniloff; 138 above left Jean Mounicq/ANA/John Hillelson Agency; 138 above right Denis Hughes-Gilbey; 138 below Jean Mounicq/ANA/John Hillelson Agency; 139 left Denis Hughes-Gilbey; 139 right Michelangelo Durazzo/ANA/John Hillelson Agency; 140 above Jean-Paul Dumontier; 140 below René Volot/ Explorer; 141 above Serge Chirol; 141 below Ciccione/Rapho; 142 Sir Terence Conran; 144 above Jean Gaumy/Magnum/ John Hillelson Agency; 144 below Jean-Paul Dumontier; 145 left Photographers' Library/ Mike Busselle; 145 right Christian Sarramon; 146 above Jean-Paul Dumontier; 146 below left Jean Gaumy/Magnum/John

Hilleson Agency; **146 below right** Jean-Paul Dumontier; **147 above** Bernard Descamps/VU; **147 below** Antoine Rozès; **148 above** Robert Estall; **148 centre** Alex MacLean/Conran Octopus; **148 below left** Sabine Weiss/Rapho; **148 below right** Raymond de Seynes; **149** Anthony Blake Photo Library; **150–151** Photographers' Library; **151 above** Anthony Blake Photo Library; **151 below** Gilles de Chabaneix; **152 above** Alex MacLean/Conran Octopus; **152 centre** Jean-Paul Dumontier; **152 below** Jean-Paul Dumontier; **153 above** Alex MacLean/Conran Octopus; **153 centre** Alex MacLean/Conran Octopus; **153 below** Michelangelo Durazzo/ANA/John Hilleson Agency; **154 above** Michelle Garrett; **154 below** Rosine Mazin/Agence Top; **155 above** Denis Hughes-Gilbey; **155 below** Michelle Garrett; **156–157** Denis Hughes-Gilbey; **157** Laurent Rousseau/Agence Top; **158 above** Denis Hughes-Gilbey; **158 below left** John Garrett; **158 below right** Guy Bouchet; **158–159** Michael Busselle; **159 left** Patrick Ward; **159 right** Denis Hughes-Gilbey; **160** Lorna Yabsley/Landscape Only; **161** Stafford Cliff; **162 above left** Philippe Perdereau; **162 above centre** Christian Sarramon; **163 above right** Denis Hughes-Gilbey; **163 below left** Christian Sarramon; **163 centre left** Jean-Paul Dumontier; **163 below right** Anthony Blake Photo Library; **163 above left** Denis Hughes-Gilbey; **163 above centre** Denis Hughes-Gilbey; **163 above right** Susan Griggs Agency/Adam Woolfitt; **163 below left** Denis Hughes-Gilbey; **163 below centre** Patrick Ward; **163 below right** Guy Bouchet; **164–165** Denis Hughes-Gilbey; **166** Christian Sarramon; **167 left** Denis Hughes-Gilbey; **167 right** Réné Burri/Magnum/John Hilleson Agency; **168** Guy Bouchet; **169 above** Raymond de Seynes; **169 centre** Guy Bouchet; **169 below left** Gilles de Chabaneix; **169 below right** Raymond de Seynes; **170 left** Tessa Traeger; **170 right** Raymond de Seynes; **171 left** Tessa Traeger; **171 right** Richard Kalvar/Magnum/John Hilleson Agency; **172 above** Bruno Barbey/Magnum/John Hilleson Agency; **172 below left** The Anthony Blake Photo Library; **172 below right** Michelle Garrett; **173** courtesy Stafford Cliff; **174–175** FAZ Magazin/Hermann Dornhege; **176 above** Hervé Donnezan/Rapho; **176 centre** Susan Griggs Agency/Adam Woolfitt; **176 below** Denis Hughes-Gilbey; **177** Raymond de Seynes; **178 above left** Patrick Ward; **178 above right** Dailloux/Rapho; **178 centre** Christian Sarramon; **178 below left** Frederic Pitchal/REA; **178 below right** Photographers' Library; **179** Tony Stone Worldwide/Jon Wyand; **180 above left** Rex Features/SIPA/Cinello; **180 below left** Moët & Chandon; **180 right** Serge Korniloff; **181** Spectrum Colour Library; **182** Sir Terence Conran; **184 above** François Halard; **184 below** Alex MacLean/Conran Octopus; **185** Charlie Waite/Landscape Only; **186** Gilles de Chabaneix; **187 above left** Pascal Hinous/Agence Top; **187 above right** François Halard; **187 below left** Christian Sarramon;

187 below right La Maison de Marie Claire/Chabaneix/Belmont; **188 above** La Maison de Marie Claire/Mounicq/Vallery-Radot; **188 centre left** Serge Chirol; **188 centre right** Anne Gaël; **188 below left** Gilles de Chabaneix; **188 below right** Jean-Paul Dumontier; **189 above** Christian Sarramon; **189 below** 100 Idées/Bouchet/Le Foll; **190** Michael Busselle; **191 above left** Christian Sarramon; **191 above right** Jean-Paul Dumontier; **191 below left** Alexandre Bailhache; **191 below right** Christian Sarramon; **192** Jean-Paul Dumontier; **193** Christian Sarramon; **194** Francis Jalain/Explorer; **195 above** The Image Bank/Hans Breedveld; **195 centre** Gary Sommer/Explorer; **195 below** Christian Sarramon; **196 above** Philippe Perdereau and Brigitte Thomas; **196 centre** Christian Sarramon; **196 below** Guy Bouchet; **197** Christian Sarramon; **198 above** The Image Bank/Francisco Hidalgo; **198 centre** Jean-Paul Hervy/Explorer; **198 below** Robert Auvin/Agence Top; **199** Charlie Waite/Landscape Only; **200 above left** Andy Hasson; **200 above right** Guy Bouchet; **200 below left** Michael Busselle; **200 below right** Guy Bouchet; **201 above** Guy Bouchet; **201 below** Francis Jalain/Explorer; **202 above** Gilles de Chabaneix; **202 below** Yves Duronsoy/Mon Jardin et Ma Maison; **203** Antoine Rozès; **204–205** World of Interiors/Jacques Dirand; **206 above** Jean-Paul Bonhommet; **206 below** Jean-Paul Dumontier; **207 above** Pascal Hinous/Agence Top; **207 below** Yves Duronsoy/Mon Jardin et Ma Maison; **208** Gilles de Chabaneix; **209 above left** Yves Duronsoy/Mon Jardin et Ma Maison; **209 above right** Christian Sarramon; **209 below left** La Maison de Marie Claire/Eriaud; **209 below right** Yves Duronsoy/Mon Jardin et Ma Maison; **210** Maison Française/Jacques Dirand; **211 above** François Halard; **211 centre** Yves Duronsoy; **211 below** Guy Bouchet; **212–213** Pascal Hinous/Agence Top (designer Jacques Granges); **213** La Maison de Marie Claire/Nico/Dhar; **214 above** Peter Baistow; **214 below** World of Interiors/Jacques Dirand; **215** World of Interiors/Jacques Dirand; **216 above** Tessa Traeger; **216 below** Gilles de Chabaneix; **217 above** Jean-Paul Bonhommet; **217 below** Yves Duronsoy/Mon Jardin et Ma Maison; **218 left** Alexandre Bailhache; **218 right** Guy Bouchet; **219 above** Christian Liaigre; **219 below** Maison Française/Jacques Dirand; **220 above** Guy Bouchet; **220 below** World of Interiors/Jacques Dirand; **221** Jean-Paul Bonhommet; **222** Sir Terence Conran; **224** Cinémathèque Française; **225 above** Jean Mounicq/ANA/John Hillelson Agency; **225 centre** Jean Mounicq/ANA/John Hillelson Agency; **225 below** Denis Hughes-Gilbey; **226 left** Derry Moore; **226 right** Ingalill Snitt; **227 left** Louis Tirilly/2ᵉ Bureau; **227 right** François Halard; **228** Agence Top; **229 above left** Mansell Collection; **229 above centre** Centre d'Enseignement et de Documentation du Costume; **229 above right** Christian Dior; **229 centre left**

Christopher Moore; **229 centre** Christopher Moore; **229 centre right** reproduced from British Vogue © The Condé Nast Publications Ltd/Lothar Schmid; **229 below** Christopher Moore; **230–231** Guy Bouchet; **232 above left** Guy Bouchet; **232 above right** Raymond de Seynes; **232 centre** Gilles de Chabaneix; **232 below left** La Maison de Marie Claire/Hussenot/Belmont; **232 below right** Antoine Rozès; **233** courtesy of Sir Terence Conran; **234** Guy Bouchet; **235 above left** Raymond de Seynes/Rapho; **235 above right** Raymond de Seynes; **235 below left** Raymond de Seynes/Rapho; **235 below right** Raymond de Seynes; **236 above left** Guy Bouchet; **236 above right** François Tetefolle/Explorer; **236 centre left** Serge Chirol; **236 centre right** Gilles de Chabaneix; **236 below left** Christian Sarramon; **236 below right** Martin Fraudreau/Agence Top; **237** Tony Stone Worldwide; **238 above** Susan Griggs Agency/Michael Boys; **238 centre** Dennis Stock/Magnum/John Hillelson Agency; **238 below** Jean-Paul Dumontier; **239** Guy Bouchet; **240** Robert Harding Picture Library/John G Ross; **241 above left** Jean-Paul Dumontier; **241 above right** Serge Chirol; **241 centre** Christian Sarramon; **241 below left** Roland Allard/VU; **241 below right** Wang Zhiping/ANA/John Hillelson Agency; **242 above left** Musée de la Publicité – Paris; **242 above centre** Michelin, France; **242 above right** Musée de la Publicité – Paris (© ADAGP, Paris 1987); **242 centre left** Musée de la Publicité – Paris; **242 centre** Musée de la Publicité – Paris (© ADAGP, Paris 1987); **242 centre right** Musée de la Publicité – Paris (© DACS, 1987); **242 below left** Musée de la Publicité – Paris; **242 below centre** Musée de la Publicité – Paris (© ADAGP, Paris 1987); **242 below right** Nicolas; **243** Musée de la Publicité – Paris (© DACS, 1987); **244 above left** Au Printemps; **244 above right** Perrier; **244 below left** Publicis Conseil, Paris; **244 below right** BSN/Branche Biscuits; **245 above** Musée de la Publicité – Paris; **245 below** Référence Saatchi Saatchi Compton; **246 above** Retrograph Archive Collection, London; **246 below** Philippe Perdereau; **246–247** BSN/Branche Biscuits; **248–251** Terry McCormick/Conran Octopus.

Translator	Anne Dobell
Text editor	Steve Dobell
House editor	Emma Russell
Assistant	Jane Hughes
Picture research	Nadine Bazar
	Jenny de Gex
Assistant	Emma Thackara
Research assistant	Barbara Poulenc-Deflandre
Designers	Kit Johnson
	David Johnson
Production	Michel Blake

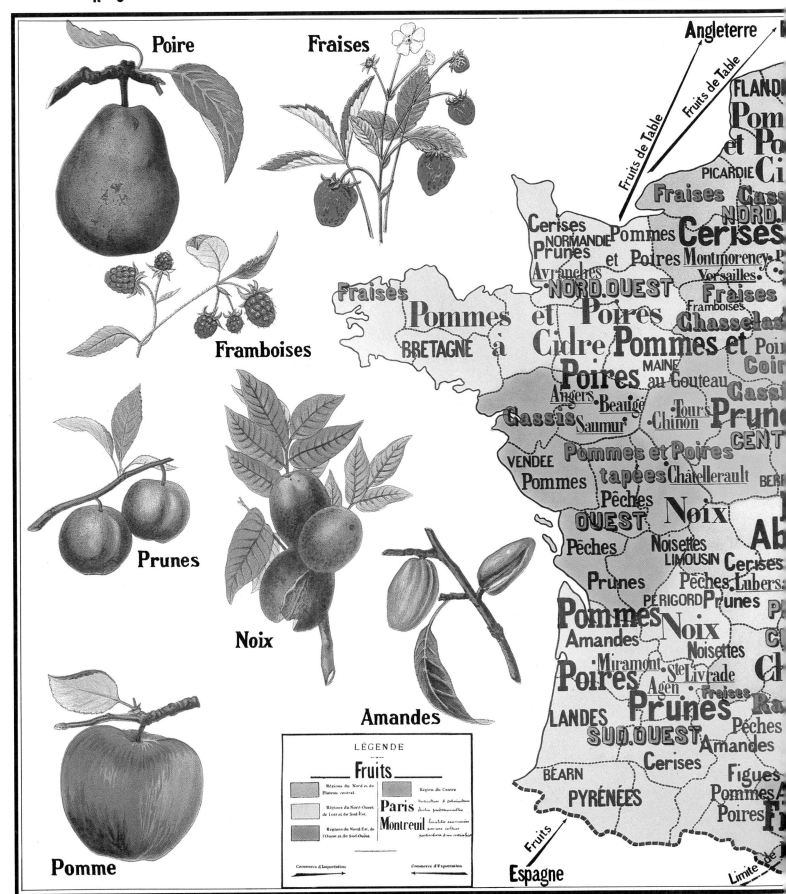

Poire

Fraises

Framboises

Prunes

Noix

Amandes

Pomme

LÉGENDE

Fruits

Régions du Nord et du
Plateau central.

Région du Centre

Régions du Nord-Ouest.
de l'Est et du Sud-Est.

Horticulture & Arboriculture
Ecoles professionnelles

Paris
Montreuil

Localités renommées
par une culture
particulière d'une certaine

Régions du Nord-Est, de
l'Ouest et du Sud-Ouest.

Commerce d'Importation

Commerce d'Exportation

Angleterre

Fruits de Table
Fruits de Table
Fruits de Table

FLAND
Pom
et Po
Ci

PICARDIE
Fraises   Cass
NORD.
Cerises   Pommes   Cerises
NORMANDIE
Prunes   et Poires Montmorency
Avranches   Versailles
NORD.OUEST   Fraises
Framboises
Fraises   Chasselas
Pommes et   Poir
BRETAGNE   à   Cidre Pommes et
Poires   MAINE   Coir
au Couteau
Angers Beaugé   Tours   Gass
Cassis Saumur   Chinon   Prune
CENT
Pommes et Poires
VENDEE   tapées Châtellerault   BE
Pommes
Pêches   Noix
OUEST
Pêches   Noisettes   Ab
LIMOUSIN
Prunes   Pêches Lubers
PÉRIGORD Prunes   P
Pommes   Noix
Amandes   Noisettes
Poires   Miramont   Ste Livrade   C
Agen   Fraises   Ch
Prunes   Ra
LANDES   Pêches
SUD.OUEST   Amandes
Cerises
BÉARN   Figues
Pommes A
PYRÉNÉES   Poires   F

Fruits

Espagne   Limite de

LES FILS D'ÉMILE DEYROL